A start me up Book

Volcanoes

By Dr. Rainer Koethe

Illustrated by Gerd Ohnesorge

Tessloff Publishing

Preface

It is a terrifying and yet fascinating sight: smoke rising from mountains that hurl sparks and red-hot rock into the air. Sometimes there are fiery streams of lava flowing from them as well. Thousands of tourists flock to extinct or dormant volcanoes like Vesuvius and Vulcano, and many also travel to see eruptions of active ones such as Etna, Stromboli, and Kilauea.

Volcanoes are a clear reminder of the powerful forces deep within the Earth. They have buried cities under ashes and killed thousands of people with clouds of hot, poisonous gas, or drowned them in tidal waves triggered by the powerful explosions. The most powerful eruptions have even affected the Earth's climate. On the other hand, the fertile, mineral-rich soil they create can often produce several harvests per year. Warmth from deep within the Earth might also supply some of our energy needs one day. It is even likely that life itself began in hot, sulphurous springs heated by subterranean forces.

Researchers have made significant progress in the past few years. Modern techniques involving sensitive measuring instruments, computers, and satellites have even made it possible to predict eruptions in some cases.

This **start me up!** ™ book describes the many phenomena that are connected to forces deep within the Earth. It presents the latest theories of researchers, tells the stories of especially devastating eruptions, and also shows how we benefit from volcanoes.

Volume 9

PUBLISHERS: Tessloff Publishing, Quadrillion Media LLC

EDITOR: Alan Swensen

PICTURE SOURCES: Archiv fuer Kunst und Geschichte, Berlin: 3r, 6 (2), 7l, 28t; Archiv Klammet, Ohlstadt: 13l; Associated Press GmbH, Frankfurt/M: 47r; Astrofoto, Leichlingen: 36r; Prof. Dr. Ernst Waldemar Bauer, Stuttgart: 37; Bavaria Bildagentur, Gauting: 11, 18l, 22l, 34, 36l, 39t; bildarchiv preussischer kulturbesitz, Berlin: 18r; Bundesanstalt f.r Geowissenschaften und Rohstoffe/U. von Stackelberg, Hannover: 43; dpa, Frankfurt/M: 8, 13r, 17, 20, 21 (2), 22r, 23, 28r, 31, 42r, 48r; Mary Evans Picture Library, London: 7r; FOCUS Bildagentur, Hamburg: 14, 15 (2), 19, 33r, 44r, 45; Helga Lade Fotoagentur, Frankfurt/M: 32/33, 40t, 42t; Historic Royal Palaces Agency, Surry: 41; IFA-Bilderteam, Munich: 15b, 16; Okapia, Frankfurt/M: 40r; Tessloff archives: 2, 3l; ZEFA Bildagentur, Dusseldorf: 1, 9, 10, 12, 22t, 24 (2), 25 (2), 33l, 35 (2), 38 (2), 39l, 40l, 42l, 44l, 47l.

COVER PHOTOS: ZEFA, Dusseldorf

ILLUSTRATIONS: Gerd Ohnesorge

Translated by William Connors

COPYRIGHT: © MCMXCVIII Tessloff Publishing, Burgschmietstrasse 2-4, 90419 Nuremberg, Germany
© MCMXCVIII Quadrillion Media LLC, 10105 East Via Linda Road, Suite 103-390, Scottsdale AZ 85258, USA

Visit us on the World Wide Web at http://www.quadrillionusa.com

Library of Congress Cataloging-in-Publication Data is available.

ISBN 1-58185-010-7

Printed in Belgium

Printing 10 9 8 7 6 5 4 3 2 1

Contents

Fire-spewing mountains have frightened people since the beginning of time ...

... but they have also fascinated them.

Fireworks From the Depths of the Earth

On October 24th in the year 79 AD a catastrophe ended the lives of many Romans living near what is now the Bay of Naples. The events of that day left the wealthy Roman port of Pompeii and eight other cities in ruins.

What cities did Vesuvius bury?

As the morning begins, however, no one suspects that a catastrophe is about to occur. The streets are full of life. Stores and bathhouses are already open. In the harbor, slaves are loading ships with jars of olive oil and wine.

Construction workers are also busy at work. There are buildings going up everywhere, since a major earthquake 13 years earlier leveled parts of the city and caused many houses to collapse. Now the villas in particular are being rebuilt in a grander style than before—after all, the money chests of the Pompeiians are well filled.

The fertile soil of the surrounding countryside and the mild climate at the edge of the Mediterranean ensure rich harvests of fruits, vegetables, and wine. But what no one knows, is that the earthquake 13 years earlier was only a warning signal for a more devastating catastrophe. After centuries of deceptive silence, destructive forces have awakened beneath the heavily forested, 5,900-foot-high Vesbius (now called Vesuvius), not far from the city.

Suddenly and without warning, disaster strikes. An earthquake

When Mount Vesuvius erupted, a cloud of poisonous, red-hot gases enveloped the Roman city of Pompeii and fragments of rock rained down. Thousands of people died in Pompeii.

again shakes the ground, followed by a thunderous bang. The peak of the mountain is blown apart in a tremendous explosion. A dark column of smoke and fire rises 15 miles into the sky. At a tremendous height, the deep black cloud spreads out across the sky like the crown of a tree and darkens the Sun. Lightning is flashing in the dark cloud. Enormous quantities of pea-sized pebbles (lapilli), pumice, and dark, ash-like sand rain down onto the frightened inhabitants.

In panic, they attempt to flee or to save their belongings. Storms of hot, poisonous sulfuric gases sweep across the city. Many people are burned or suffocated and buried in the layer of ash that is now many feet deep and covers streets and houses, fields and vineyards. Heavy rains fall and mix with the ash, forming enormous rivers of mud. One such mudflow pours over the neighboring town of Herculaneum. The gray-brown wall of mud moves slowly through the streets, knocking down doors and windows, filling every room and burying the city under a 50-foot layer of mud that will soon harden like concrete.

In the course of the catastrophe, at least 12,000 people lose their lives, villages and cities within a radius of 12 miles are completely destroyed. When the clouds finally clear several days later and the Sun breaks through, the survivors discover only a few roofs and columns jutting out of the mud and rock.

Over the centuries these once prospering cities fell into oblivion. Fortunately, however, we have a written account of the unfolding of this disaster. Pliny the Elder, a naturalist and admiral of the Roman fleet, died in the catastrophe. His nephew was an eyewitness to the calamity and recounted his uncle's death to the historian Tacitus. Tacitus' writings still exist for us to read. It wasn't until about 250 years ago, however, that someone accidentally stumbled upon the ruins of these cities. Since then archaeologists have been working to excavate these sites.

Much of what we know about Roman life comes from the work of archaeologists who have examined the remains of Pompeii and Herculaneum. The layers of ash and mud protected the ruins from weathering, and even preserved jewelry, furniture, scrolls (Roman "books"), statues, murals, mosaics, tools, and various articles for everyday use. Workers even found charred bread in ovens they uncovered. Thanks to these excavations,

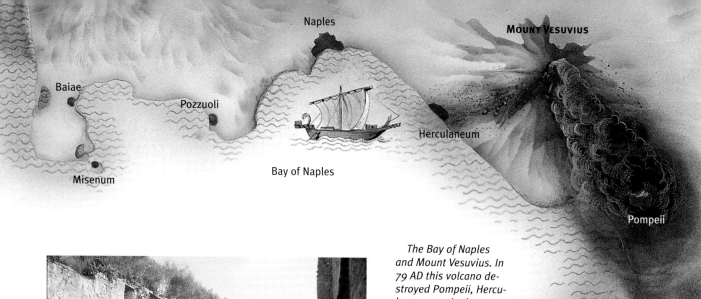

Naples

MOUNT VESUVIUS

Baiae

Pozzuoli

Herculaneum

Bay of Naples

Misenum

Pompeii

Sorrento

The Bay of Naples and Mount Vesuvius. In 79 AD this volcano destroyed Pompeii, Herculaneum, and other towns.

This excavated street in Pompeii was the site of inns, shops, and houses.

we can again wander through the streets of Pompeii and Herculaneum, past theaters and bathhouses, bars and stores, villas and small workshops.

The layer of ashes even preserved some of the inhabitants. Although the bodies had completely decomposed, the hardened ash preserved "molds" of them. Archaeologists poured plaster into these hollows and obtained good likenesses of people caught in the disaster.

Vesuvius has erupted several times over the centuries, the last time in 1944. Since then there has been silence, but it is a deceptive silence. The forces within the Earth could awake at any time and threaten the approximately four million people who live around the Bay of Naples.

The wall mosaics have been partially preserved in this house of a wealthy Roman in Herculaneum.

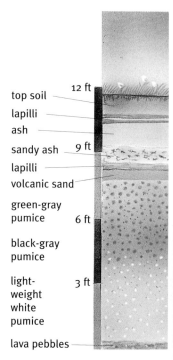

top soil — 12 ft
lapilli
ash
sandy ash — 9 ft
lapilli
volcanic sand
green-gray pumice — 6 ft
black-gray pumice
light-weight white pumice — 3 ft
lava pebbles

About 12 feet of volcanic rock and ash covered Pompeii.

HERCULANEUM was once a rich seaside resort. Prosperous Romans decorated their houses with mosaics and sculptures. At first, archaeologists excavating the city believed that only few people had died in the catastrophe. In 1980, however, several hundred skeletons of men, women, and children were discovered under the floors of boat houses, where they had apparently tried to hide.

How did the ancient Greeks and Romans explain volcanoes?

Fire-spewing mountains have fascinated and frightened people since the beginning of humankind. Many peoples thought they were the homes of gods, and that the gods were expressing anger through the fiery eruptions. Some cultures even tried to appease the gods by offering human sacrifices. Even today, many inhabitants of the volcanic island Hawaii make sacrificial offerings of flowers, tobacco, and fruits to the goddess Pele, who is said to live on Kilauea volcano, in its large, fiery lakes of molten rock.

The ancient Greek and Roman myths explained the smoke escaping from volcanoes as smoke from the underground fires of the god Hephaestus (the Romans called him Vulcan), who forged weapons and armor for the gods with the

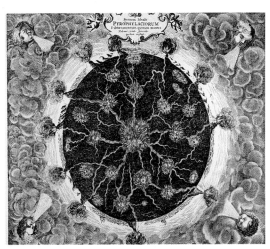

In the 17th century, some people believed that huge fires deep within the Earth fueled the volcanoes.

involve the gods. They believed there was a powerful fire burning in the depths of the Earth, fueled by combustible materials like sulfur. Only a few centuries ago, some scientists believed that huge burning coal deposits fueled the fires of volcanoes. We now know that the reality of volcanoes is much more complicated than this, but also much grander than the scholars of ancient times imagined. Even today, however, the name we give these fire-spewing mountains—"volcano"—reminds us of the ancient stories of the gods.

Where does the enormous power of volcanoes come from?

The diameter of the Earth is about 7,900 miles from pole to pole. Its surface—the part we live on—is only a thin crust less than 50 miles thick. This crust covers a huge ball of molten rock. There is no coal burning in its depths, however. The heat comes primarily from radioactive materials that occur naturally in rock. When their atoms decompose, they release heat just as a power plant does.

This 2,600-year-old Greek vase shows the return of Hephaestus to Mount Olympus.

help of one-eyed giants—the Cyclopes. When Hephaestus became angry, he hurled red-hot rock and fire out of the chimney.

Scholars in the ancient world looked for explanations that didn't

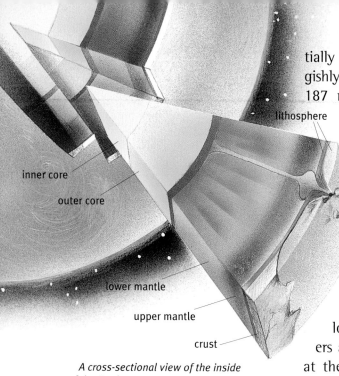

inner core

outer core

lithosphere

lower mantle

upper mantle

crust

A cross-sectional view of the inside of the Earth.

Normally this tremendous heat is kept within the Earth by its outer layer, the crust.

Although it is impossible for humans to travel into the interior of the Earth, we have a fairly good idea of the structure of our globe. The core of the Earth is composed of metal, primarily iron and nickel. Even though the temperature of the inner core is about 9,000° F, it remains solid because of the tremendous pressure from the layers of metal and rock above it. Surrounding the inner core is the outer core, an ocean of molten iron and nickel with a temperature between 6,700 and 8,300° F.

The next higher layer is the mantle. Unlike the core, which is made of metals, the mantle is composed of a mixture of rocks and minerals. Like the core, it also has two layers. Again, because of tremendous pressure, the rock of the lower layer is solid despite a temperature of 5,500° F. The temperature in the outer mantle is about 2,700° F and the rock is par-

tially melted here and flows slug-gishly. The upper mantle is about 187 miles thick. Above it is the crust on which the oceans and continents rest.

The force of volcanoes originates in the upper mantle. It isn't the typical, semi-melted rock of this layer that rises in volcanoes, how-ever. The rock of the up-per mantle is not uniform and some elements melt at lower temperatures than oth-ers and are therefore liquid even at the temperatures of the upper mantle. These elements are also lighter than the surrounding vis-cous rock and press upward like huge bubbles several miles in di-ameters.

We call this hot, molten rock magma (Latin for "kneaded mass"), and its temperature is be-tween 1,650 and 2,700° F. Often it collects in immense magma cham-bers, where it presses out against the surrounding rock and partially melts it. If the pressure from gases in the magma is especially great, or if the crust above the magma al-ready has cracks or crevices, the magma is able to escape to the surface: a volcano erupts.

EARTHQUAKES
give us a glimpse into the Earth's inner structure. Every earthquake sends seismic waves (a kind of sound wave) through the globe, and these waves are recorded by seis-mometers around the world.

THE SEISMIC WAVES
behave differently in the dif-ferent material of the Earth's inner layers, and the waves are also "bent" when they pass from one layer to anoth-er—as light waves passing through glass are bent —for example, from the upper man-tle to the lower mantle. By measuring the changes in the waves, scientists can form a kind of x-ray of the Earth.

Showers of sparks and rivers of lava light up the night sky during an eruption of Mount Etna.

Gases, ash, lapilli

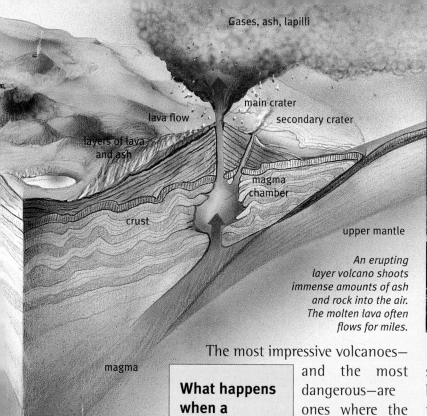

main crater

secondary crater

lava flow

layers of lava
and ash

magma
chamber

crust

upper mantle

*An erupting
layer volcano shoots
immense amounts of ash
and rock into the air.
The molten lava often
flows for miles.*

magma

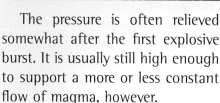

WHEN VOLCANOES ERUPT, they sometimes form searing clouds of gases and ash that pour down the slopes of the volcano at speeds of up to 300 miles per hour. A cloud like this suffocates and burns everything in its path—it moves so fast that it is impossible to escape.

In 1902 a hot, poisonous cloud like this poured down from **MT. ST. PELÉE** onto the city of St. Pierre and turned it into a smoking wasteland within a few minutes. Only one person survived the catastrophe—a prisoner protected by thick prison walls. Even behind these walls, however, he was severely injured. Twenty-eight thousand people died.

The most impressive volcanoes—

What happens when a volcano erupts?

and the most dangerous—are ones where the liquid rock is expelled with explosive force. The magma of such volcanoes contains high levels of dissolved gases. As long as the rock masses above press down on the magma, the gases remain dissolved in the melted mass. If the magma finds a way up to the Earth's surface, however, the pressure decreases and the gases are released. They then blow the magma out of the volcano in a glowing column of fiery rock that sometimes reaches miles into the sky. Glowing rock fragments crash to the ground on all sides of the eruption site.

The tremendous force of the eruption atomizes some of the magma into fine droplets. They solidify during their flight through the air and rain down as black or reddish-brown sand and dust. Because of its color this dust is often called volcanic "ash"—a reminder of the old belief that there were coal fires burning in the deep.

The pressure is often relieved somewhat after the first explosive burst. It is usually still high enough to support a more or less constant flow of magma, however.

As soon as magma comes out of the Earth, it is called lava. Like a red-hot river, this liquid rock cuts a path down the mountainside. The lava slowly cools and changes its color from white-hot (more than 3,600° F) to yellow, then bright red, then dark red, and finally to black (below 1,000° F). Woe to any trees or houses in the path of the lava flow—the extreme heat incinerates them within seconds. Finally, the cooled lava hardens to brown-black stone—sometimes miles away from the place where the lava first came out of the Earth.

The gases released in the explosion are just as dangerous as the boulders raining down or the rivers of molten rock. There are large quantities of water vapor and carbon dioxide, as well as poisons such as hydrogen chloride (hydrochloric acid in gaseous form), hydrogen fluoride, sulfur dioxide, and hydrogen sulfide, which smells like rotten eggs.

Volcanic Cones, Lava Flows, and Showers of Stone

Occasionally scientists have an opportunity to watch a volcano being created. On the afternoon of February 20, 1943, the Mexican farmer Dionisio Pulido saw just such a terrifying event with his own eyes. He was working as usual in his field when a large crack suddenly appeared in the ground. Smoke and steam came out of the crack accompanied by thunderous rumblings. Then sparks flew up and set trees on fire. He immediately ran back to his village, Paricutin, and warned the other villagers. In the meantime the subterranean forces in the crevice were raging more and more fiercely. A

black column of smoke rose higher and higher, sparks flew, lightning flashed, and red-hot boulders were hurled into the air. The next day, there was a cone 164 feet high where previously there had been a level field. A new volcano was born. Two days later lava began to flow out of the volcano and after a week the mountain had reached a height of about 490 feet. The thundering eruptions could be heard more than 185 miles away—and ash particles rained down this far away as well. The following year, lava flows covered the village of Paricutin and several neighboring villages as well. Not until 1952 did the volcanic forces subside. In the course of these 9 years, the Paricutin

Do all volcanoes have the same shape?

Mount Fuji has erupted about 15 times since 781 AD. Its last eruption was almost 300 years ago.

MOUNT FUJI is located near Tokyo and many Japanese consider it a sacred mountain. Its cone has a nearly perfect classical volcano shape. The mountain rises 12,388 feet and usually has snow at its top in the winter. For the Japanese, Mount Fuji embodies the "beauty, grandeur, and power of all of nature."

volcano had grown to a height of about 1,500 feet.

Most volcanoes are formed in this way. This is why they have similar shapes: a volcano is usually a cone-shaped mountain, composed of discharged ash and cooled lava. The peak does not form a sharp point as is often the case with other mountains, but instead forms a hollow basin, the crater. If the volcano is active, a shaft, the vent or chimney, leads from the crater down into the Earth's depths. Sometimes magma forces its way to the surface through other channels and new vents open up on the volcano.

Not all volcanic cones look the same, however. There are some with steep slopes and others with very gentle slopes. This depends on the composition of the magma.

In addition to the temperature of the magma, the most important factor is its content of gases and silicic acid. Silicic acid is the same element that makes up quartz, the main component of many rocks and sand. The gas content determines the pressure with which the

Looking across the crater basin of Halemaumau toward Mauna Loa, a shield volcano on the island of Hawaii.

magma bubbles or shoots out of the crater. Silicic acid determines how fluid the magma is. The more silicic acid the magma contains, the more slowly it flows. When the percentage of silicic acid is more than 65 percent, we talk about acidic magma. The temperature must reach 2,190° F or higher before it will melt. It flows only very slowly, like toothpaste or putty, and quickly hardens when exposed to air. If the percentage of silicic acid is below 50 percent, we call the magma alkaline. It melts already at temperatures below 1,830° F, and it flows rapidly. Lava flows originate from volcanoes fed

HALEMAUMAU is an immense, circular collapsed crater on Hawaii. The Hawaiians believed the volcano goddess Pele lived in it. There has not been any lava for about 60 years, but there are explosions with powerful discharges of ash from time to time. These explosions are caused by ground water seeping down to the hot magma where it immediately turns to steam.

Depending on the composition of the lava, volcanoes develop different shapes.

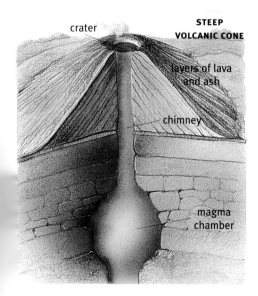

crater

layers of lava and ash

chimney

magma chamber

STEEP VOLCANIC CONE

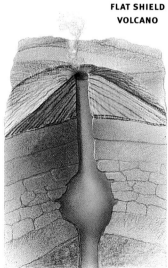

FLAT SHIELD VOLCANO

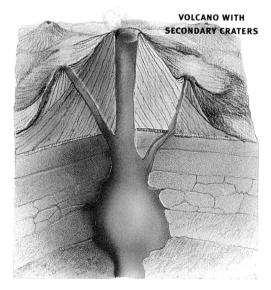

VOLCANO WITH SECONDARY CRATERS

by alkaline magma. Their liquid magma can flow for miles before it hardens. Close to the crater, it can reach speeds of more than 150 feet per minute. The fastest lava flow ever recorded moved at speeds of about 35 miles per hour—in other words, about 3,000 feet per minute.

Lava of low viscosity (thickness) normally flows quite smoothly out of the throat or "vent" of the volcano and spreads over a wide area. Over time a low, flat hill is formed, shaped like a warrior's curved shield lying on the ground. This type is therefore called a "shield volcano." Mauna Loa on Hawaii has such a shape. It rises "only" 13,678 feet above the Pacific. This is only the upper part, however, and the gently sloping sides of this massive volcanic mountain continue down another 16,400 feet under water. At its base on the ocean floor, Mauna Loa has a diameter of more than 180 miles. From its base on the ocean floor to its peak above the ocean, this volcano is taller than Mount Everest in the Himalayas, which measures 26,906 feet from base to peak and is the highest point on Earth.

On the layer volcano Mount Ngauruhoe on New Zealand you can see the dark beds of old lava flows.

When the magma is rich in gases and silicic acid volcanoes form cones with steep slopes. Loose materials expelled by the volcano (ashes, small rocks, and large boulders) build up and are covered again and again by layers of lava. Specialists call this a "layer volcano." Many famous volcanoes—Vesuvius, Etna, Stromboli, and Fujiyama—belong to this type.

Finally, there are also volcanoes that are not mountains. From time to time quickly flowing, alkaline lava wells up out of crevices or fissures that may be many miles in length. The lava flows out in such huge quantities that valleys and whole landscapes are flooded by

IN EARLIER PERIODS OF THE EARTH'S HISTORY there have been very large expulsions of lava. In the South American Paraná basin, which encompasses southern Brazil, northern Argentina, Paraguay, and Uruguay, hardened lava up to 1,900 feet deep covers an area more than twice the size of California.

A layer volcano is formed by alternating discharges of lava and ash. The tremendous quantities of steam released in such an explosion lead to heavy rainfalls.

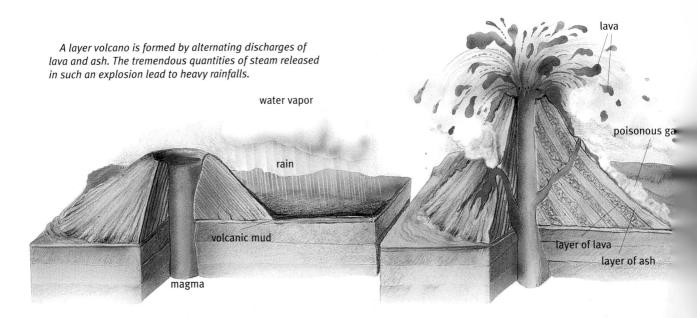

water vapor

rain

lava

poisonous gas

volcanic mud

magma

layer of lava

layer of ash

A flat volcanic cone located on the Laki Fissure on Iceland. Huge amounts of lava were expelled here in 1783.

Do volcanic eruptions create new land?

In 1963 a new island called Surtsey was created in the waters south of Iceland. On the morning of November 14th, the crew of the fishing boat Isleifur II was puzzled by a strange cloud of smoke over the ocean. They sailed toward it and saw volcanic ash and red-hot rock shooting up. Within a few hours, the smoke column reached more than 13,000 feet

In 1963, the volcanic island of Surtsey gradually rose out of the sea near Iceland, accompanied by smoke and fire.

THE PEOPLE OF ICELAND have an especially close relationship with their volcanoes. More volcanoes exist there than anywhere else on Earth. There have been many eruptions that have devastated large areas of land. The whole island is made of volcanic rock, and without its volcanoes—there are more than 100—it would not exist.

the molten rock. In 1783, the inhabitants of the North Atlantic island of Iceland experienced the largest such eruption in recorded times. Within a three-month period, more than 2.8 cubic miles of lava flowed out of a 15-mile fissure, the Laki Fissure. The lava flowed up to 40 miles away from the opening. At the same time, volcanic gases escaped and spread across the country, poisoning grass and killing livestock. The eruption resulted in a famine in which more than 10,000 people died, one fifth of the island's population.

into the air, and thick clouds of steam were bubbling up from the water. The next day, a small, black island had formed and was already 30 feet high. Violent eruptions continued, and it grew rapidly. One month later it had risen 460 feet above the water.

Volcanic activity on Surtsey has since subsided. The island is not yet inhabited, but biologists visit it regularly. For them it is a very interesting laboratory. They can observe here how plants and animals slowly take possession of new volcanic land.

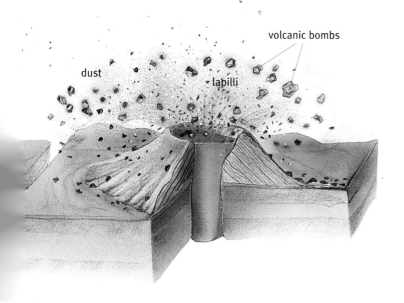

dust

lapilli

volcanic bombs

13

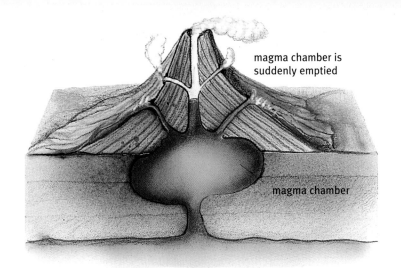

magma chamber is suddenly emptied

magma chamber

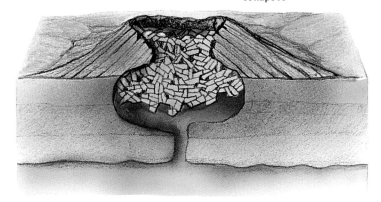

cone of the volcano collapses

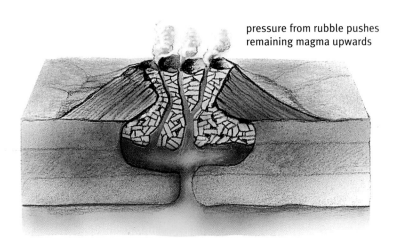

pressure from rubble pushes remaining magma upwards

What is a caldera?

If the magma chamber is emptied very quickly by powerful gas eruptions, the peak of the volcanic cone may collapse. We call a greatly enlarged volcanic crater like this a "caldera" (the Latin word for "cauldron" or "pot"). When Vesuvius erupted in 79 AD, for example, it lost its peak and along with it about 6,000 feet in height. The peak became a caldera. On volcanic islands the ocean sometimes seeps into the caldera, often leaving only shreds of the previous volcano rising out of the water. In the case of volcanoes on the mainland, rainwater often collects in the caldera, creating a lake. This is how Crater Lake on Mount Mazama in Oregon was formed. The mountain erupted about 6,500 years ago and its caldera has a diameter of almost six miles and a depth of 3,700 feet.

The caldera of an extinct volcano, Mount Mazama, filled with water to form Crater Lake.

Volcanic activity doesn't usually end with the forming of a caldera, however. After a few years, a new volcano forms in the middle of the giant basin. Thus there is a small volcanic cone in the middle of

Crater Lake—now a small, forested island. The volcano we now call Vesuvius actually stands in the middle of the caldera that was created during the eruption in 79 AD. Monte Somma, near the present cone of Vesuvius, is the highest point in the old caldera's rim.

After an eruption, the cone collapses and a caldera is created. It isn't long until smoke starts pouring out of new vents, however.

Pahoehoe lava often forms smooth, rope-like folds before it solidifies completely.

The surface of aa lava is made of rough, sharp-edged fragments.

What shapes does hardened lava take?

VOLCANIC TUFF

When the loose material discharged by layer volcanoes—ash, pebbles or lapilli, and dust—solidifies and finally turns to rock, we call this rock volcanic tuff. Volcanic tuff is a popular construction material, since it is relatively soft and therefore easy to work. It is also good insulation.

Reddish-brown volcanic tuff is a popular construction material.

The island of Hawaii is a particularly good place to observe volcanic activity. The lava pouring from the volcanoes there is relatively thin and flows very quickly. It makes its way almost peacefully and without explosion until finally it solidifies. Consequently, volcanologists—and tourists too—can get close to the craters, lava flows, and lava lakes without danger. Hardened lava is a common sight for Hawaiians. They even coined words for the different forms lava takes when it hardens, and volcanologists have adopted these words as scientific terms.

The hot, thick soup of molten rock can solidify in a number of very different ways. If lava with a high temperature and low viscosity wells up slowly, a black skin forms on the surface of the lava flow after only a few yards due to cooling. Sometimes a flow gets stuck, and then bulges and folds form, sometimes looking rather like cow droppings. Scientists call this kind of lava pahoehoe (pronounced "puh-HO-eh-ho-eh"), which in Hawaiian means "lava you can walk barefoot on." It is so smooth that it won't cut bare feet.

The skin that forms on the surface as the lava cools is good insulation and keeps the molten lava below from cooling. It now flows like water in a pipe. If the lava supply is interrupted but the molten rock continues to flow out the lower end, the "pipe" may run dry. This can leave mile-long lava caves that are several yards high and wide. One such tunnel, the Thurston Tube on Hawaii, is nearly 16 feet across at its widest point. On the island of Lanzarote in the Canary Islands one enterprising businessman even built a tavern in the mouth of a lava cave.

Aa (pronounced "AH-ah") lava has very different characteristics. It is made up of sharp-edged, angular, twisted blocks of slag that cause painful cuts in bare feet—and hands, if you fall on it. It gets its name from the cry of pain you let out when you step onto it or fall on it. It can even shred sturdy shoes in a very short time.

Aa lava is created when large amounts of gas escape the lava as it is expelled, so that bubbles rising through the thick lava throw fragments into the air, creating fountains of rock. The fragments thrown up harden into rough pieces called clinker. The lava can no longer flow smoothly, and now pushes forward with difficulty and breaks up into many rough pieces in the process. These are either carried onward with the flow, or they fall in front of the flow and it pours over them. A flow of aa lava looks like a heap of glowing clinker slowly pushing forward.

A third kind of lava, pillow lava, is found in huge quantities at underwater volcanoes. It is created when lava is expelled underwater. The sudden cooling creates a bag-like formation with a hard crust. The pressure of the lava below pushes it out of the fissure. It separates from the flow and solidifies into the shape of a pillow.

What is igneous rock?

200 years ago, geologists were engaged in a heated debate over the origin of the rocks we find on Earth today. The "Neptunists" (named after the Roman ocean god Neptune) claimed that all varieties of rock came from the sea, including gray basalt, for example. The "Plutonists" (named after Pluto, the god of the underworld), on the other hand, claimed that all rock types were formed in the fiery center of the Earth. They were squeezed out through cracks in the Earth's surface or spewed up by volcanoes. They then solidified.

We now know that both camps of scientists were in part right. There are types of rock that arose in the sea, for example, sedimentary rocks like limestone and sandstone. Igneous (Latin: "from fire") rocks, on the other hand, are formed when molten rock—magma—cools and solidifies.

This doesn't have to happen on the Earth's surface, nor is a volcano always necessary. The pressure and heat of the magma aren't always intense enough to break through the Earth's crust. If the pressure subsides after a while, then the magma solidifies beneath the surface. It cools very slowly here, protected by the layers of rock above it. During this slow cooling the various elements of the magma separate out and collect into individual crystals. We can recognize this type of igneous rock—called "plutonic" or "intrusive" igneous rock—by the grainy texture created by these crystals.

The best-known intrusive rock is granite, a popular stone for use in building since it is beautiful and very hard. Depending on its composition it may be gray, reddish-brown, or green. Intrusive rock can also reach the Earth's surface when the rock above it has been eroded by wind and rain over the millions of years of the Earth's history.

When magma reaches the surface and solidifies quickly, on the other hand, it forms "extrusive" igneous rock. This kind of rock is very fine-grained and has a uniform structure since the various elements of the magma didn't have time to separate. The most important representative of this type of rock is basalt, a hard, gray rock. A lot of basalt was formed in the sea, but not in the way the Neptunists thought. It is formed from magma that squeezes through cracks in the ocean floor and then solidifies.

Under certain conditions, BASALT forms hexagonal columns as it cools and solidifies. These columns look like organ pipes packed together. A good example of this is the "Giant's Causeway" on the northern coast of Ireland, a row of hexagonal basalt columns. They are up to 20 feet high and about 15 to 20 inches in diameter.

"Giant's Causeway" on the northern coast of Ireland reaches down almost 600 feet into the sea.

PUMICE is created when a shower of free-flowing, gas-saturated magma is suddenly blown into the air. The gases are released from their dissolved state and form bubbles, causing the lava to foam. It quickly solidifies, forming a light, porous rock—so light that it even floats on water.

Fire-Spewing Mountains and Towering Fountains

Violent eruptions of the Plinian type often occur after the volcano has been silent for centuries. Mount St. Helens is this type of volcano. It blew off more than 1,000 feet of its peak when it erupted on May 25, 1980.

Every volcano behaves differently, and volcanoes can also change their behavior over the years. Some volcanoes are very

Can volcanoes explode?

unpredictable and are considered particularly dangerous. Volcanologists distinguish five basic types, distinguished especially by the gas content of the magma and by its type of flow. The most harmless type of volcano is the Hawaiian type. Lava from this type of volcano has a low gas content and flows freely. Although it usually flows in large quantities, it does so

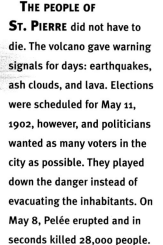

Volcano of the Hawaiian type

THE PEOPLE OF ST. PIERRE did not have to die. The volcano gave warning signals for days: earthquakes, ash clouds, and lava. Elections were scheduled for May 11, 1902, however, and politicians wanted as many voters in the city as possible. They played down the danger instead of evacuating the inhabitants. On May 8, Pelée erupted and in seconds killed 28,000 people.

peacefully and without explosive noises from the crater. It forms huge shield volcanoes. If the silicic acid content of the magma is high and its viscosity (thickness) as well, it solidifies easily and may clog the vent. In volcanoes of the Strombolian type this leads to frequent but not very powerful explosions. Whenever sufficient gas pressure builds up in the magma under the solidified areas, it blasts away the thin crust. This type is named after the Stromboli volcano, located on a Mediterranean island north of Sicily. It erupts like this every 20 to 30 minutes and throws sparks, lava bombs, lapilli, and ashes a few yards up into the air. It is comparatively harmless as long as you don't get too close.

While Hawaii lava flows somewhat like honey, magma from volcanoes of the Pelean type is more like tar. The name comes from a volcanic mountain on the Caribbean Island of Martinique. In 1902 it erupted, destroying the port city of St. Pierre. Its thick magma solidifies very easily, forming a tight "cork" in the throat of the volcano. Every once in a while, gas pressure pushes this cork of hardened lava out of the throat and several hundred yards into the air. It looks like it is growing out of the crater.

The "cork" of a Pelean Volcano is lodged so tightly, that even very high gas pressure in the rising magma can't loosen it. Eventually, the gas seeks another route to the surface, usually on the side of the cone—with

The ruins of St. Pierre after the eruption of Mount Pelée.

Volcano of the Strombolian type and a photograph of the volcano it is named after.

Volcano of the Pelean type

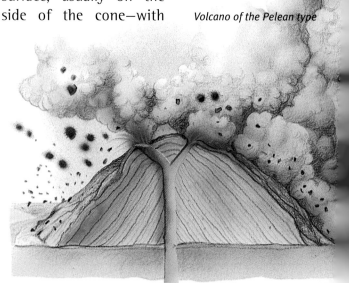

The crater of Stromboli. It erupts every 20 to 30 minutes, but the eruptions are comparatively harmless. Here the volcano crater erupts in two spots at the same time.

devastating results. A searing cloud of ashes, rock fragments, and smoke rushes down the mountainside at a speed of more than 300 miles per hour and spreads for miles across the land. No one knows in advance if and when such a fiery avalanche will occur or what course it will take. The rapid tempo of the events leaves no time for flight. This is why volcanoes of the Pelean type are considered so dangerous.

The magma from volcanoes of the Plinian type—named after Pliny the Elder, who was killed when Vesuvius erupted in 79 AD—also frequently clogs the vent, since it is rich in silicic acid and very thick. In this type of volcano, however, the rising gas pressure eventually blows the cork out of the vent with an explosion that destroys everything around it. After this initial catastrophe, the mountain continues to erupt violently for several days and hurls out great quantities of ashes, volcanic bombs, and lava.

Centuries of quiet may pass between such periods of eruption. These long dormant periods are what make volcanoes of the Plinian type so dangerous. For a long time the volcano seems to be extinct. The slopes become green with vegetation and are often used for agriculture. Villages and cities

Volcano of the Krakatoa type

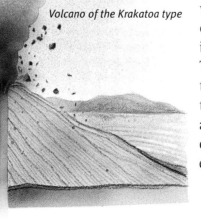

rise up in the surrounding countryside. Eventually, however, the forces within the Earth reawaken. The inhabitants of Washington State experienced such a reawakening in 1980 when Mount St. Helens erupted and blew away its peak, devastating the landscape for miles around. It had been dormant for more than a century.

In the case of Vesuvius, the dormant periods have been even longer. It had been dormant for 800 years before it buried Pompeii and Herculaneum. It was quiet for 600 years before it erupted violently in the year 1631, burying the city of Portici. To make sure people didn't forget this, the viceroy of Naples had a warning sign posted among the ruins of Portici, offering the following advice to later generations: "Children and grandchildren! Beware! Sooner or later this mountain will catch fire. Before this happens, however, you will hear thunder, roaring, and earthquakes. It will spew forth flames, smoke, and lightning. The air will quiver, rumble, and howl. Flee while you can. Don't worry about house and hearth, just flee without a moment's hesitation."

But as devastating as volcanoes of the Plinian type are, they are occasionally surpassed by volcanoes of the Krakatoa type. If the magma is very thick and the pressure deep within the Earth very great, the eruption may be so explosive that it blows the entire volcano to bits. The sound can often be heard thousands of miles away, and at times its effects may even be felt around the globe. One of the worst catastrophes of this type was the explosion of Krakatoa.

Krakatoa is a volcanic island in the Sunda Strait between the Indonesian islands of Java and Sumatra. In the year 1883, after more than 200 years of silence, it erupted violently—several times. These explosions were only the prelude. On August 27, 1883, it exploded with inconceivable force. A column of fire and ash shot up at least 30 miles into the sky—five times as high as jet planes fly. Pumice rained down hundreds of miles away. The thunderous explosion was heard as far as 3,000 miles away—about the distance between New York and London! The captain of a ship 26 miles away reported that the eardrums of half of his crew had burst.

A gigantic tidal wave was responsible for the greatest number of casualties, however. It was caused by the collapse of the magma chamber beneath the volcano. It devastated the coasts of the surrounding islands, destroyed almost 300 cities and villages, and killed more than 36,000 people. It even caused damage in San Francisco harbor—on the other side of the Pacific, more than halfway around the globe. For years, winds carried dust from the explosion around the globe, causing unusually colorful sunsets. A thick layer of floating pumice hampered ship traffic in the Sunda Strait for years. All that was left of the former island were bare stretches of land. It was a long time before anything grew there again.

Krakatoa's volcanic forces have not been extinguished, however. In

Anak Krakatoa around 1952, 69 years after the devastating Krakatoa explosion.

1927 a new volcano appeared out of the sea near the original island. It was named Anak Krakatoa (son of Krakatoa) and has since continued to grow taller and wider—fed again and again by new eruptions. Perhaps it will also explode in a few centuries, as Krakatoa did. Krakatoa, too, grew up among the ruins of a volcano that had exploded thousands of years earlier.

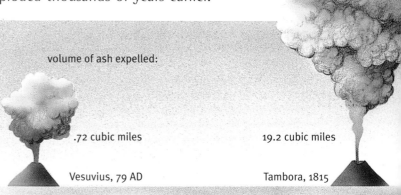

volume of ash expelled:

.72 cubic miles

Vesuvius, 79 AD

19.2 cubic miles

Tambora, 1815

For much of the Northern hemisphere, the year 1816 became known as the "year without a summer." The summer temperatures recorded on the east coast of the United States and in Europe were the lowest in over 200 years. Many crops froze, and cold waves brought frost and snow as late as July. The resulting

The amount of ashes expelled isn't always a measure of the force of an eruption.

NEXT TO PREHISTORIC ERUPTIONS, even Krakatoa and Tambora seem like harmless fireworks. In Yellowstone National Park, for example, there is a giant caldera about 40 miles wide. It was created by volcanic eruptions some 600,000 years ago.

famines forced many people to leave their homes and move to more fertile regions.

What they didn't know, was that this unusual weather was the result of a volcanic eruption in faraway Indonesia. Mount Tambora on Sumbawa Island had erupted in April of 1815, and its eruption was much more powerful than Krakatoa 70 years later. With the accompanying earthquakes, thunderstorms, and tidal waves, the eruption cost more than 90,000 people their lives. The eruption removed 4,500 feet of the mountain's height, and left behind a caldera four miles across. The Earth shook within a radius of about 1,000 miles, and, according to eyewitnesses, clouds of ash darkened the Sun as much as 300 miles away. In the United States this would be like an eruption in

Enormous clouds of smoke, gas, and ash rise from Pinatubo volcano in the Philippines in 1991.

Washington, D. C. darkening the sky over New York City and causing the ground to tremble in Miami, Florida.

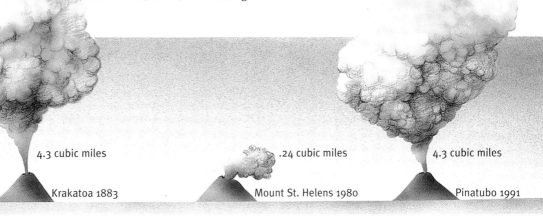

4.3 cubic miles

Krakatoa 1883

.24 cubic miles

Mount St. Helens 1980

4.3 cubic miles

Pinatubo 1991

El Chichón appears peaceful now, but in 1982 it sent clouds of sulfuric gas around the globe.

The amount of ash expelled into the atmosphere was inconceivable. For years, ash clouds drifted around the globe at high altitudes, absorbing some of the Sun's light and causing below-normal temperatures around the world. As destructive as the effect of volcanic ash is, it does not compare with that of sulfuric acid clouds. They block a greater part of the Sun's rays and for a longer time. Scientists discovered this in 1982, when the Mexican volcano El Chichón erupted. It hurled very little ash into the air, but it blasted great quantities of sulfuric gas 15 miles up into the sky. Chemical reactions transformed the gas into a dense cloud composed of minute drops of sulfuric acid. They didn't just absorb the sunlight, they also reflected it back into space. Using special satellites, meteorologists were able to observe the way the cloud expanded and slowly covered the entire Northern hemisphere and part of the Southern hemisphere. Since the El Chichón eruption was quite weak compared to the Tambora or Krakatoa explosions, the average temperature sank only a bearable 0.5° F.

The hot springs of Pamukkale in Turkey have created a fairyland of travertine.

How are hot springs formed?

When the forces of the deep awaken, it does not always result in a volcano. Often the magma remains underground and cools there very slowly. It transfers its heat to the surrounding layers of rock. If ground water flows through these rock layers, it heats up and rises to the surface as hot springs—also called thermal springs. Frequently the hot water dissolves minerals from the rock layers it flows through: calcium, sodium chloride (table salt), sulfur, iron, or magnesium, and usually carbonic acid.

The water in hot springs often has a high calcium content. Calcium carbonate deposits called "travertine" develop around the edges of these springs, forming beautiful terraces and water-filled basins. This travertine is often gleaming white, but it is not unusual to find it colored by traces of other minerals. The travertine formations at the Turkish springs of Pamukkale have been known since ancient times, and the springs were a popular bathing site for the Romans. The travertine terraces and basins at Mammoth Hot Springs in Yellowstone National Park are even larger. Bacteria and algae color the edges of many of the hot springs a shiny yellow, orange, or red. Each kind of algae settles in water of a specific temperature.

The travertine formations at Mammoth Hot Springs in Yellowstone National Park.

Volcanic forces heat this bubbling, sulfurous mud near Beppu, Japan.

MINERAL WATER often has beneficial effects for our health. It is bottled for drinking and used for mineral baths. Spas offering mineral baths were very popular in the United States and Europe in the 19th century—Saratoga Springs, New York was one of the most famous sites in the United States for mineral baths.

The geysers at Yellowstone National Park are certainly among its most spectacular sights. Geysers are springs that discharge jets of steam and water high into the air, usually at irregular intervals—although in some cases with astonishing regularity. Seeing a geyser is an unforgettable experience. At first, the spring simply bubbles and steams. Then the water swells up, and suddenly a glistening column of steam and water shoots high into the air, accompanied by loud hissing and roaring noises. Springs like this can be found in many places throughout the world. The name "geyser" comes from the Icelandic word "geysir," meaning "to rush forth."

It was only about 150 years ago that scientists discovered how geysers work. At sea level, water normally boils—turns to steam—at 212° F. If you increase the pressure

Hot water and steam shoot out of dozens of geysers in Yellowstone National Park.

on the water, however, the boiling point—the temperature at which water boils—rises. The neck of a geyser is like a pipe extending hundreds or even thousands of feet into the ground. Ground water seeps into it through cracks and fills it. Magma trapped under the ground heats the water. The column of water in the "pipe" pushes down on the water below and raises the pressure on it. It can now reach temperatures well above

What are geysers?

THE "GREAT GEYSER" near Haukadalur, Iceland is considered the grandfather of all geysers. It has been dormant for many years, however. No one knows why it stopped or if it will start again, but its neighbors are still active.

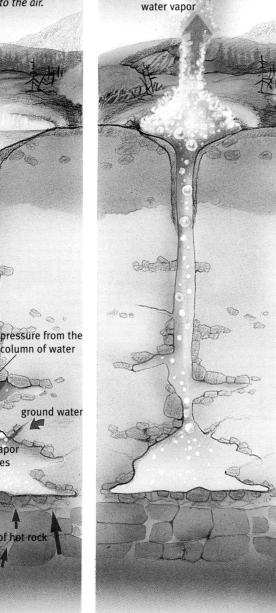

Cross-section of a geyser. At regular intervals hot water vapor propels the column of water up into the air.

water vapor

pressure from the column of water

ground water

water-vapor bubbles

layers of hot rock

A solfatara crater on Iceland. There is actually a lot more water vapor rising from the crater than you can see.

Heated by volcanic forces, sulfurous water vapor rises continually from this spring.

212° F without turning to steam. If water at the top of the pipe is removed, however—as it heats up it expands and spills out of the narrow pipe—the pressure below drops, and the superheated water at the bottom instantly begins to boil, violently and explosively. This pushes the upper column of water out of the pipe, shooting it up as high as 160 feet.

Another striking phenomenon at Yellowstone National Park are the many clouds of steam hissing out of the cracks in the Earth. The steam often contains sulfuric compounds that form deposits of delicate, bright yellow sulfur crystals around the openings. If the temperature of this steam is above 390° F, we call the vent a fumarole. If the steam contains sulfur, the vent may be called a "solfatara" (Italian for "sulfur place"). You should never reach into one of these vents, since the steam would scald your hand in-

What is a fumarole?

stantly, and it often contains caustic or poisonous substances.

Normally we don't notice the huge amounts of water vapor discharged by fumaroles, since water vapor itself is invisible. It only becomes visible fog when it comes into contact with cool air and condenses into fine water droplets.

The characteristics of water vapor also explain something called the "solfatara phenomenon." If you wave burning newspaper back and forth near a solfatara that seems to be producing only a little steam—tour guides often do this for tourists—huge clouds of thick fog immediately form. For a long time this was a puzzle, but today we can easily explain it. Although the superheated, invisible vapor cools when it comes in contact with air, it can only form water droplets if it finds something to condense on—a "condensation nucleus," for example, fine dust or ash particles. Smoldering paper creates large quantities of such particles. This trick demonstrates just how much water vapor is actually coming out of the Earth here.

WHEN VOLCANOES GROW DORMANT and stop adding new material, erosion immediately begins eating away at them. Ash and stone rubble are soon washed away. Layers of hardened lava last longer, but in the end only the solidified magma in the volcano's chimney remains—creating beautiful columns like Devil's Tower in Wyoming (picture, page 35).

What happens when a volcano becomes extinct?

Volcanoes don't last forever. After a volcano cools down, wind and rain begin to erode its surface. When subterranean volcanic activity ceases—and with it the pressure from the magma—volcanic islands often sink back into the ocean under their own weight. Sunken volcanoes are especially common in the South Seas. Thanks to the untiring activity of small sea animals called corals, we can often see the sites of former island volcanoes. These creatures constantly excrete calcium, forming huge coral reefs on these sunken volcanoes.

Corals apparently love extinct volcanoes because of the nutrients the ocean washes out of the rock. As the former volcano sinks more and more, the reef grows higher and higher. In the end all that is left is a ring-shaped coral reef—an atoll. If it sticks out of the water, the ocean may deposit sand on it and palm trees may even take root.

The final sign of an extinct volcano is the discharge of carbon dioxide. This is the gas that forms bubbles in carbonated drinks. It is not poisonous, but when it occurs in large quantities it displaces the oxygen in the air and can cause suffocation. In the Dog Grotto near Naples, for example, this gas is constantly seeping out of cracks in the rock. It is heavier than air and settles on the cave floor in an invisible three-foot layer. Adults and tall children can enter the grotto without danger, but small children and dogs would suffocate.

1,400-foot-high Ship Rock in the New Mexico desert. It, too, is a solidified volcanic chimney—the cone of the volcano was eroded away.

Millions of tiny animals— corals—build strange and colorful structures out of calcium. Over time, they create huge coral reefs in this way.

Why did people die at Lake Nyos?

Although carbon dioxide gas is harmless when compared to a volcanic eruption, it can still cause catastrophes—as "killer lakes" in Cameroon in West Africa have shown. These are crater lakes in a region once actively volcanic. Vegetation has long since made the hilly landscape green again. The lakes are still, but death lurks within. On the evening of August 21, 1986, a giant column of steam and water rose out of one of these lakes, Lake Nyos. It poured down the sides of the volcano and filled the surrounding valleys. Within a few minutes, almost 2,000 people and thousands of animals were dead. The invisible cloud of carbon dioxide had suffocated them.

What happened? For some time, carbon dioxide had been seeping through cracks in the rocks and dissolving into the water. Large quantities of dissolved gas built up in the water at the bottom of the lake. The colder the water and the higher the pressure exert-

active volcano

Mid-Oceanic Ridge

direction of plate movement

Eurasian Plate

Juan-de-Fuca Plate

PACIFIC OCEAN

Philippinian Plate

Pacific Plate

RING OF FIRE

Indo-Australian Plate

INDIAN OCEAN

Dissolved carbon dioxide (CO2) in the water at the bottom of the lake made Lake Nyos a "killer lake."

ed on it, the more gas it can dissolve. In the Lake Nyos, the water nearer the surface pressed down on the water below, increasing its capacity to absorb carbon dioxide.

The water at the bottom was colder and therefore heavier than the surface water, and so it stayed at the bottom. Then a slight earthquake caused part of the volcano's rim to collapse into the water, and this stirred up the deep water. The carbon dioxide held in the water as carbonic acid (carbonation) bubbled up and flowed over the rim of the crater into the valleys below.

water pressure

old volcano

build-up of dissolved CO_2 in deep water

CO_2 (carbon dioxide gas) seeps in through cracks in surrounding rock

poisonous cloud of CO_2 gas

CO_2

minor earthquake causes a landslide

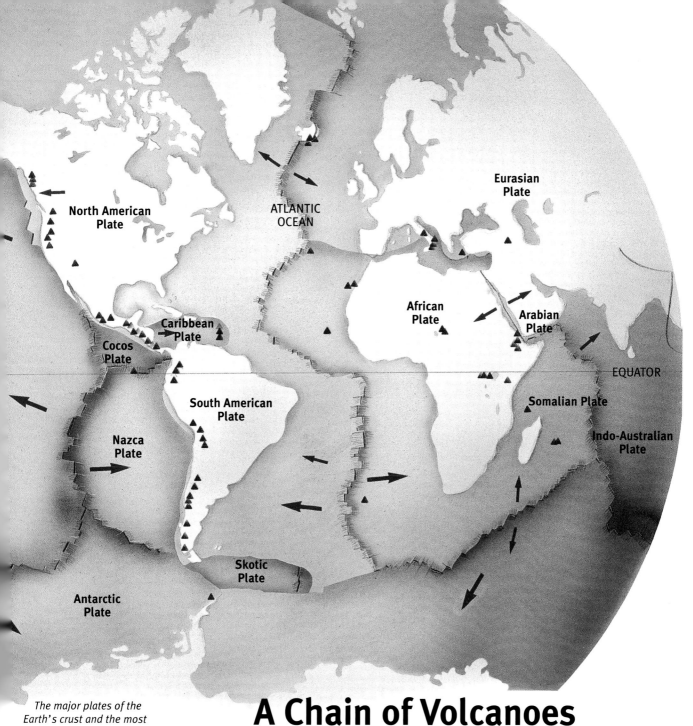

The major plates of the Earth's crust and the most active volcanoes.

A Chain of Volcanoes

Why are there so many volcanoes along the Pacific coasts?

On every continent there are volcanoes that belch forth smoke, even on ice-covered Antarctica. American geologists have worked hard to compile a list of all the volcanoes that are active, or that have been active during the last 10,000 years. Their catalog lists 1,511 volcanoes and 7,886 documented eruptions. Of these eruptions, 86 were so powerful that the crater collapsed into a caldera. There are about 500 volcanoes still active today. Although Europe has the fewest of all the continents with 77—and half of these are on Iceland—the volcanoes around the Mediterranean provide researchers

27

with very important data. People have been observing and recording the activity of these volcanoes for centuries. We have precise data on 232 eruptions of Mount Etna alone.

The great majority of volcanoes are located along the coasts of the Pacific Ocean. There are more than 1,000 encircling the Pacific like pearls in a necklace. This "Ring of Fire" forms a giant horseshoe. It starts in New Zealand, passes through the islands of the South Seas, through Indonesia and the Philippines to Japan and all the way up to the Russian peninsula Kamchatka. It crosses the Bering Straits as the Aleutian Arc and then passes through Alaska, along the west coast of Canada and the United States, and extends all the way down Central and South America to Tierra del Fuego ("Land of Fire").

Many of the volcanoes in this chain are notorious. Some have killed thousands of people, such as Mayon and Pinatubo in the Philippines, Krakatoa and Tambora in Indonesia, and Mount Fuji, Japan's sacred mountain. On the east coast of the Pacific there are Mt. St. Helens in Washington; Popocatépetl, Paricutin, and El Chichón in Mexico; and Nevado del Ruiz and Villarrica in the Andes Mountains.

For a long time geologists were puzzled by the fact that volcanoes weren't evenly distributed around the globe, but instead formed conspicuous chains limited to certain areas. The chain of volcanoes along the coast of the Pacific isn't

Meteorologist and explorer Alfred Wegener formulated the theory of continental drift.

the only one. There are strings of volcanoes in other parts of the globe, for example, in the Caribbean, on Iceland, on Hawaii, along the Mediterranean, and in East Africa.

Geophysicist, meteorologist and polar researcher Alfred Wegener (1880 – 1930) was the first scientist to take the right track in solving this mystery. He wasn't really interested in volcanoes, however. He was intrigued by the fact that the facing coasts of the African and South American continents look like separated parts of a puzzle. Although they are now separated by thousands of miles, they look as if they once belonged together. Wegener concluded that the continents were slowly drifting across the Earth's surface, somewhat like icebergs on the open sea.

When Wegener published his theory of continental drift in 1912, it immediately drew worldwide attention. Most geologists rejected the theory, however. At that time, they were convinced that the positions of the continents and oceans hadn't changed much since the beginning of time. Above all, Wegener couldn't identify a force capable of moving huge continents across the Earth's surface. Since the mid-20th

The San Andreas Fault in California is at the "seam" between two continental plates.

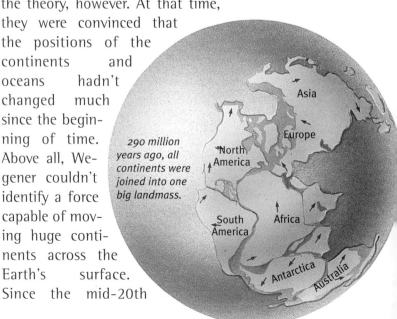
290 million years ago, all continents were joined into one big landmass.

Asia
Europe
North America
South America
Africa
Antarctica
Australia

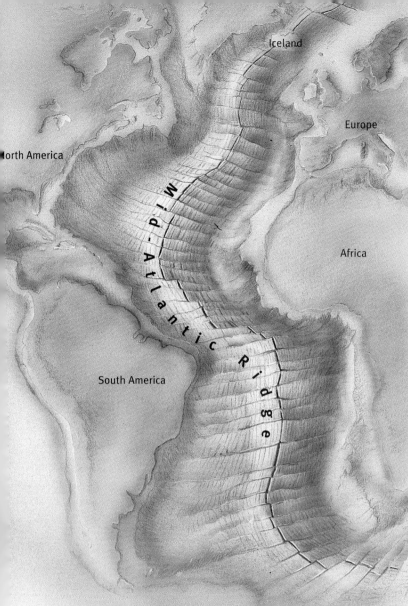

The Mid-Atlantic Ridge—one part of the Mid-Oceanic Ridge—passes through the Atlantic. Iceland is part of this huge volcanic zone where magma is constantly rising to the surface.

ones, each up to 60 miles thick. These plates "carry" the continents and the ocean floors—the Pacific plate, for example, carries the Pacific Ocean. The continents are actually nothing more than the highest parts of these plates—the parts that are above sea level. They are composed of lighter rocks than the deeper parts of the plates and so they always remain on the surface.

How do the continental plates move?

The continental plates are moving at speeds of a few inches per year, and all are moving in different directions. The continents, of course, move with them. Their movement is a little like that of ice floes on the ocean. Instead of floating on water, however, the plates "float" on the semi-liquid rock of the Earth's upper mantle. Currents in this sea of hot rock cause the plates to move. As the deepest layers heat up, they rise, and the cooler masses above sink and are heated in turn. Thus the Earth's inner fire keeps this sluggish "sea" in motion.

Sometimes subterranean forces pull two plates apart. Here fiery magma from the Earth's mantle flows up through the gap and solidifies into basalt rock. New plate material is continually being formed in this way. These huge masses of basalt have also created the longest mountain range on Earth. It is also the least known, however, since nearly all of it lies below the surface of the oceans. It runs underneath all of the oceans and is called the Mid-Oceanic Ridge. It is over 43,000 miles

MODERN RESEARCH SHIPS have provided a lot of evidence supporting the theory of plate tectonics. They drill deep into the ocean floor and take core samples of the rock. Analysis of these samples shows that the upper layers of the ocean floor are relatively young basalt. As the plates along the Mid-Oceanic Ridge move apart, magma surges up and hardens into basalt—creating new ocean floor.

century, however, geologists have made many discoveries that support Wegener's theory. Exploration of the ocean floor has yielded particularly strong evidence.

Today we call the theory of continental drift "plate tectonics" (from Greek tektonikos, meaning "related to construction"). When geologists began studying the ocean floor with modern measuring instruments, they discovered that the Earth's crust is broken up into a mosaic of seven large "plates" and more than 20 smaller long—more than one-and-a-half times the Earth's circumference! It is about 900 miles wide and up to 10,000 feet high. In a few places it sticks up through the ocean's surface. The volcanic island of Iceland is part of the Mid-Oceanic Ridge. The volcanoes and crevasses on Iceland show us that Europe and North America are drifting apart here at a rate of about 0.8 inches per year. Given the size of the continents, 8 tenths of an inch isn't very much. Over time it adds up, however. Over the past two million years, the Atlantic has become about 25 miles wider.

The Mid-Oceanic Ridge is the longest chain of volcanoes on Earth. It is basically nothing more than a 43,000-mile-long crack from which magma is constantly flowing. The flow is harmless, however. This isn't just because ocean water immediately cools it and stops violent eruptions. Above all it is because there isn't much silicic acid in the molten rock rising through the crevices, and the lava therefore flows freely.

The Earth's surface cannot grow endlessly. When new plate material is created in an expansion zone, plate material somewhere else must disappear. Where two plates collide,

for example, one of them disappears beneath the other. It is pressed down into the hot mantle at an angle of about 45 degrees and eventually melts. An area like this is called a subduction zone. The forces of the deep are especially apparent here. Earthquakes are common in these zones. The reason for this is again the movement of the plates. One plate doesn't simply slide smoothly under the other. The rough edges catch and it moves in fits and starts. With each jerk, the Earth quakes. The number of volcanoes formed in subduction zones is also very high.

Subduction volcanoes are often

Which volcanoes are the most treacherous?

time bombs waiting to go off. Almost all notorious volcanoes are located in subduction zones. Beneath Krakatoa and Tambora, the Indo-Australian Plate pushes under the Eurasian Plate. Pinatubo and Mayon are located above the

THE ANDES MOUNTAINS on the west coast of South America were created when the Nazca Plate was forced under the South American Plate and pushed down into the upper mantle. The rock of the downward-moving plate melts in the depths of the Earth, and lighter elements push upward through the plate above. This leads to earthquakes and intense volcanic activity. In the Central Andes there are rock layers from ancient eruptions that are thousands of meters thick.

This cross-section of the ocean floor shows the most important types of plate movement: at left is an expansion zone, in the center a plate pushes over a hot spot, and at right one plate moves underneath another (a subduction zone).

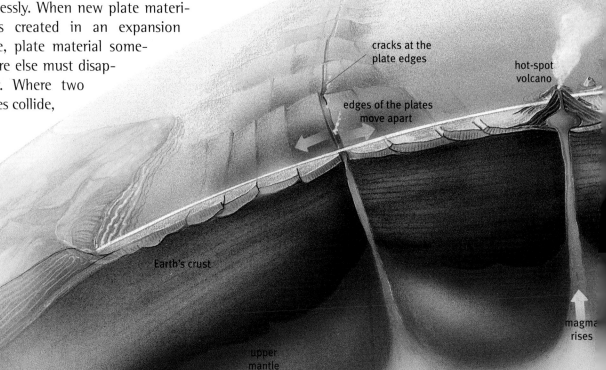

cracks at the plate edges

edges of the plates move apart

hot-spot volcano

Earth's crust

magma rises

upper mantle

People fleeing during the eruption of Pinatubo in 1991. Fine ash made it difficult to see or breathe.

area where the Philippine Plate disappears beneath the Eurasian Plate. The eruption of Pinatubo in 1991 was the most powerful one in this century, not only in explosive force, but also in the quantity of ash it disgorged. It buried 200,000 acres of farmland and more than 20 towns.

The reason these volcanoes are so dangerous lies in the composition of their magma. It contains high levels of silicic acid and dissolved gases. The levels are especially high in places where the lower plate pushes down under a plate that supports a continent, as is the case on the west coast of the United States. Geologists suspect that the lower plate drags a large piece of the ocean floor with it—in other words, rock containing water. At a depth of about 60 miles—and beneath the other plate—the rock begins to melt. The glowing magma created in the process is rich in gases, including water vapor. The gases come primarily from the rock dragged down from the ocean floor. This magma now seeks a path toward the surface. In doing so it penetrates the rock of the continental plate. Unlike the oceanic plates, continental plates contain high levels of silicic acid. The magma pushing upward dissolves some of it out of the rock and absorbs it.

The silicic acid makes the magma more viscous, however. As a result, when it finally reaches the vent of a volcano, it frequently blocks the opening. If the pressure of the gases then rises, it forces the blockage out in a devastating explosion—as happened in 1980 at Mount St. Helens in Washington State.

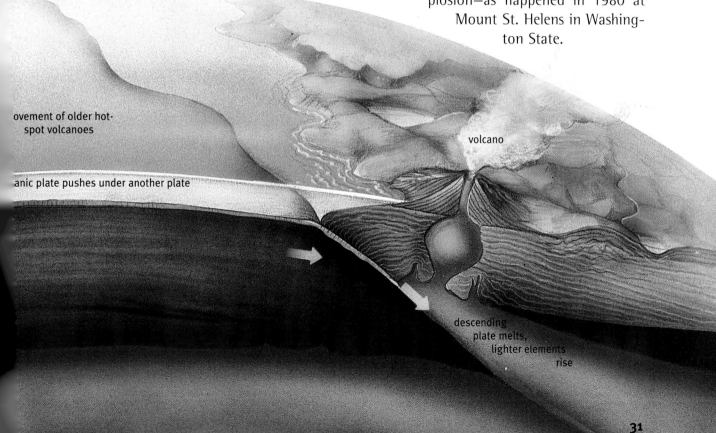

ovement of older hot-spot volcanoes

anic plate pushes under another plate

volcano

descending plate melts, lighter elements rise

Along the Pacific coast of the United States, where the small Juan-de-Fuca Plate pushes under the North American Plate, the continental plate has buckled and folded, forming the Cascade Mountains. Here, beneath the surface, enormous magma chambers feed a chain of 15 volcanoes. Among them are Mount Rainier, forever sending up smoke; Mount Hood, with its smell of sulfur; Mount Mazama, with Crater Lake; and Mount St. Helens, presently the best-known and most notorious of them all. Volcanologists have studied the explosion of Mount St. Helens on May 18, 1980 more thoroughly than perhaps any other eruption. They knew very well how dangerous the volcanic vents in the Cascade Range are. Consequently, they placed numerous monitoring devices in this area, and these devices automatically transmitted their data to Vancouver, Canada. Finally Mount St. Helens signaled the start of renewed activity with a number of earthquakes. The earthquakes didn't do much damage, but volcanologists knew what they meant. Officials sealed off a large area around it, and there were almost no people in the extensive forests around the volcano when it erupted.

It began with a landslide. A week before the eruption, the rising magma had pushed up against the north slope, creating a bulge. This now broke free and slid down the mountain, taking with it huge

The volcanic peaks of the Cascade Mountains are considered particularly treacherous.

Mt. Baker

Glacier Peak

Seattle

Mt. Rainier

Mt. St. Helens

Mt. Adams

Mt. Hood   Columbia River

PACIFIC OCEAN

CASCADE MOUNTAINS

Mt. Jefferson

Three Sisters

Newberry Caldera

Mt. Thielsen
Crater Lake/Mt. Mazama

Mt. McLoughlin

Mt. Shasta

Lassen Peak

quantities of rocks and ice from the peak. This created a sudden drop in the pressure bearing down on the magma chamber, and the trapped gases expanded violently and blew off the peak. Gigantic black clouds of smoke, gas, and ash shot sideways and upwards out of the mountain, followed by pumice stone, and tremendous quantities of ash. The lateral eruption caused the greatest destruction. More powerful than a hurricane, this hot, glowing cloud—with a temperature of 500° F—swept across the forests, flattening them over an area of 230 square miles and setting them on fire. Soon

On the left you can see Mount St. Helens after it erupted. On the right is the snow-capped peak of Akutan volcano, one of the most active Alaskian volcanoes. The most recent activity from Akutan was in 1992 when it spewed steam and ash in plumes that rose as high as 15,000 feet.

The explosion of Mount St. Helens (1980) destroyed millions of trees, knocking them down like toothpicks.

after this, an avalanche of more than 100 billion cubic feet of mud, ash, ice, and tree trunks poured into the valleys and lakes and filled them with up to 590 feet of this material, leaving behind a vast, lifeless desert.

Nevertheless, thanks to the foresight of public officials "only" 57 people died during the eruption of Mount St. Helens. An eruption of Nevado del Ruiz in 1985 demonstrated the importance of taking warnings seriously. Beneath this volcano, the Nazca plate pushes under the South American plate. Scientists announced an impending eruption, but no one reacted. Then, on November 13, it happened. The volcano didn't actually discharge any great amount of ash, but the heat from the blast melted part of the ice fields on the 17,716-foot-high peak. Enormous rivers of mud ("lahars") raged down the slopes, filling the valley with a flow of gray mud that reached to the tops of the houses. The rivers of mud continued down the bed of the Lagunilla River with unstoppable force. Finally, two hours later and 30 miles on down the valley, the flow buried the town of Armero under a layer of mud several feet deep. Twenty-five thousand people died. A simple warning system might have saved their lives.

Mount St. Helens isn't the only dangerous volcano on the West Coast. Its neighbor, Mt. Rainier, could easily send similar deadly mudflows into densely populated areas. It is currently considered the most dangerous candidate in the Cascade Mountains. Although it is presently quiet, geologists watch it carefully. In the past 10,000 years, its lava has melted the surrounding glaciers more than 60 times, causing huge mudflows that poured into neighboring rivers. It blew off its entire peak 5,700 years ago—sending almost one cubic mile of ash and rock into the valley of the White River. Immense mudflows

Are other volcanoes on the west coast of the United States dangerous?

even reached Puget Sound. A similar eruption could devastate Seattle and other surrounding towns.

The other volcanoes in the Cascade Range are also considered time bombs, from Lassen Peak in California—with its boiling mud ponds—all the way north to Mount Garibaldi in Canada. No one knows when one of them—Mount Hood, Mount Baker, or Mount Shasta—will awake from its present sleep. Geologists therefore monitor these volcanoes constantly.

The Pacific Ring of Fire continues north and runs along the south coast of Alaska over to Asia. Perhaps the most dangerous volcano in Alaska is the Katmai. In 1912 it expelled more than 4 cubic miles of ash within a two-day period and literally buried Kodiak Island. Where the peak had once been there was now only a gaping caldera three miles wide. The river of lava that poured out of the crater flowed into a long, narrow valley, which has been known ever since as the "Valley of Ten Thousand Smokes."

How did the Hawaiian volcanoes originate?

Not all volcanoes form at the edges of tectonic plates. Roughly one in ten forms in the middle of a plate. The Hawaiian volcanoes are examples of this type. They are part of a chain of volcanic islands in the middle of the Pacific Ocean on the Pacific plate.

These volcanoes were formed by something volcanologists call "hot spots." Magma bubbles seem to rise from great depths almost constantly at these hot spots. Because of its high temperature, the molten rock melts the thin crust under the ocean and breaks through to form a volcano. The plate that the magma broke through isn't fixed, however—it is moving at a speed of an inch or two a year. As a result, the

The freely flowing lava of Hawaiian type volcanoes is discharged without any great roar and flows away quietly.

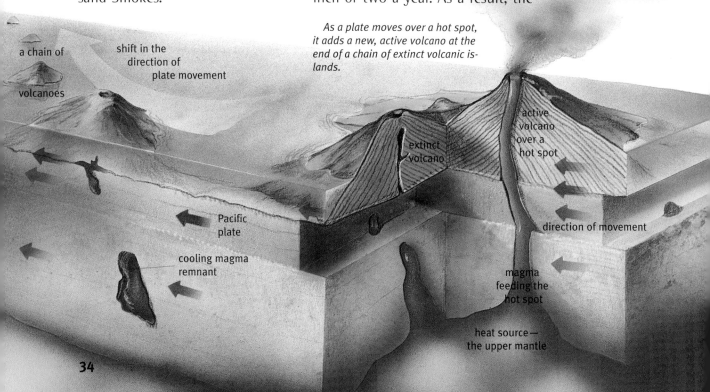

As a plate moves over a hot spot, it adds a new, active volcano at the end of a chain of extinct volcanic islands.

a chain of
volcanoes

shift in the direction of plate movement

extinct volcano

active volcano over a hot spot

Pacific plate

direction of movement

cooling magma remnant

magma feeding the hot spot

heat source— the upper mantle

Devil's Tower in Wyoming

DEVIL'S TOWER in Wyoming is a witness to former volcano activity. A volcano belched out smoke here about 60 million years ago. After it became extinct, the magma in the chimney solidified, creating beautiful columns. Erosion carried away the surrounding earth while the rock remained and formed the 867-foot-high mountain. Theodore Roosevelt declared it a national monument in 1906.

volcano is slowly cut off from its magma source and then becomes extinct. A few miles away, however, a new volcano will form in the same way. The hot spot is directly under the currently active volcano. From the chain of extinct volcanoes left behind, we can see the direction of the plate's movement.

The Hawaiian Islands demonstrate this very clearly. The Pacific plate is moving in a west-northwesterly direction. At present, the hot spot is located under the Kilauea volcano. The next volcano to the northwest, Mauna Kea, has become more and more quiet, and the volcanoes of the other Hawaiian Islands are clearly extinct. Once the magma stops feeding these volcanoes, their tremendous mass begins pushing these basalt cones slowly into the ocean floor. Wind, weather, and ocean surf are eating away at them as well. The Hawaiian volcanic chain actually continues underwater farther to the northwest, but the remains of the former volcanoes no longer jut out of the ocean. Hot spot volcanoes are fed by freely flowing alkaline lava and are consequently rather harmless.

Of course, hot spots aren't just found under the oceans. Mount Etna on Sicily is probably fed by a hot spot, and hot magma also rises up through the continental plate in the Yellowstone region. The Yellowstone hot spot is already very old. It was already under the area of America's first national park about two million years ago. At that time, it exploded in one of the biggest volcano eruptions of the Earth's history. It spewed out more than 540 cubic miles of magma, enough for 6 or 7 large volcanic mountains! It erupted again 1.3 million years ago with twice the force of the first great eruption. A third series of eruptions produced about one thousand times as much lava as Mount St. Helens did in 1980. The last big eruption was 70,000 years ago, but geologists expect there are more to come. As beautiful as the park is, with its geysers, mudholes, colorful thermal springs, and travertine basins, and with its rich animal and plant life, the ground beneath it holds forces that could quickly reduce everything within a wide radius into an ash-covered desert.

Yellowstone National Park is located above a volcanic "basement."

Are there volcanoes on other planets?

In 1971, the space probe Mariner 9 entered an orbit around Mars and transmitted pictures of the Red Planet back to Earth. Some of them held a sensational discovery: they showed a group of immense volcanic cones, much more powerful than any on Earth. The largest has been given the name Olympus Mons. Its gigantic base measures 373 miles in diameter—about five times larger than the biggest volcano on Earth, Mauna Loa in Hawaii. It is also more than twice as high. Mauna Loa is about 32,800 feet from base to peak—although only 13,678 feet of this height rises above the ocean's surface; Olympus Mons is 88,600 feet high. Its caldera alone is larger than most volcanoes on Earth with a diameter of 53 miles.

As its flat slopes show, Olympus Mons is a shield volcano. This would also explain its size. It produced lava for about 200 million years, but also stayed at the same place since there are no drifting plates on Mars. It appears to be extinct today.

Only three of the planets and moons in our solar system still have active volcanoes: Earth, Venus, with its atmosphere containing huge clouds of sulfuric acid, and sulfur-covered Io, one of Jupiter's moons. Information sent back by the Voyager space probes suggests that Io is the most unusual moon in our solar system. When astronomers saw the first pictures of Io they were amazed. Instead of a surface scarred by craters, the pictures showed a speckled, reddish brown landscape with ragged-edged, gleaming white fields and very dark spots. It

A volcanic eruption on one of Jupiter's moons, Io. The fountain of sulfur compounds is more than 50 miles high.

looked like a pizza with melted cheese. The most surprising picture showed a bright cloud that was shaped like an opened umbrella. It was the first time humans had witnessed a volcanic eruption on another planet.

In the meantime, scientists have discovered that the volcanoes on Io spew out immense amounts of sulfur and sulfur compounds, and that the entire moon is covered with deep sulfur deposits.

ASTRONOMERS have not observed any volcanic eruptions on Venus yet, but its atmosphere is full of sulfur compounds that could only come from volcanoes. Due to temperatures around 1,100° F at ground level, the discharged sulfurous materials evaporate quickly or are chemically transformed.

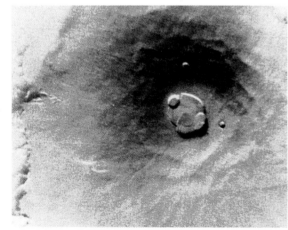

88,600-foot-high Olympus Mons on Mars is the largest known volcano in our solar system.

Living with Volcanoes

A farmer on Lanzarote, one of the Canary Islands, spreads black, volcanic ash on his field. On Lanzarote they call this ash Picon. During the night it absorbs dew and enriches it with minerals before passing it on to the soil below. During the day it stores the sun's warmth.

Why do people settle near volcanoes?

Given the devastating volcanic catastrophes and the thousands of deaths they cause, you might think that volcanoes are one of the greatest dangers human beings face. In comparison to the number of people killed in traffic accidents and by smoking, or by other natural disasters such as earthquakes and tornadoes, the number of deaths due to volcanoes is very small. Volcanic eruptions do, of course, cause terrible suffering but now, as in ancient times, people seem to keep their fear of these fiery mountains within limits. Even on the slopes of Mount Etna—at 10,902 feet the highest active volcano in Europe—farmers have built villages and established fields and vineyards. The inhabitants always fled when the mountain threatened to erupt, but as soon as the volcano was quiet again they always returned to their fields covered with ash and lava. They did so because of the fertile volcanic soil. The ashes hurled out of volcanoes contain important plant nutrients such as phosphorus, potassium, and calcium. In earlier times people were more dependent on such soils, since there were no chemical or artificial fertilizers. Harvests were often so small that many

These grapevines on Lanzarote grow in plots covered with black, volcanic ash and enclosed by low walls.

people starved. It only takes a short time for volcanic ash to become fertile soil that can yield two to four harvests per year in mild climates. Furthermore, high mountains collect water from clouds and there are usually numerous springs near the base of the mountains. At the base of Mount Etna, for example, farmers are able to grow lemons, oranges, and tangerines. At an altitude of 2,300 feet there are vineyards growing on the slopes, and also fig, almond, and olive trees. At 3,300 feet wheat fields spread across the slopes, and even further up there are cherry, apple, and pear orchards and also chestnut trees.

In the Atlantic, on one of the Canary Islands—Lanzarote—the inhabitants make use of yet another of the beneficial qualities of volcanic ash—its ability to store mois-

ture. Lanzarote has no high mountains to catch rain-clouds—none of the volcanic cones rises higher than 2,000 feet. As a result, water is in high demand. Farmers therefore cover the fertile humus soil of their fields with a thin layer of black volcanic ash. During the night the ash absorbs dew and passes this water on to the soil, along with nutrients. During the day, the ash absorbs heat from the Sun. To protect the plants from drying winds, the farmers plant them in sunken beds surrounded by low stone walls.

As destructive as volcanic eruptions are, people still manage to derive benefits from these forces. From volcanoes we get basalt and porphyry for use in construction; a kind of natural glass called obsidian; metallic ores; raw chemical substances like sulfur and cinnabar (a mercury compound); and even some gemstones.

What is volcanic rock used for?

Basalt is an extremely hard type of rock and was once broken up and used to pave roads—prisoners often had to do this strenuous work. Today machines grind it up and then mix it with tar to make durable asphalt for roads. At temperatures above 2,200° F basalt melts and can be drawn out into fibers. This basalt "wool" won't

LANZAROTE is a popular tourist spot today. Starting in 1730, volcanic eruptions covered the most fertile part of the island with black, brown, and red ash. The area is now a nature reserve, but you can enter it on special buses or by camel. At one spot, tour guides throw a piece of paper into a hole and it bursts into flame because of the intense heat rising from the Earth.

Because basalt is extremely hard, it makes good cobblestones.

SULFUR is important to the chemical industry. In earlier days people used primitive ovens to melt sulfur out of volcanic rock. It starts to melt at 230° F. In more recent times, geologists have discovered immense subterranean deposits of sulfur in several places around the world. The sulfur is extracted in open-pit mines. Another method pumps superheated water into the deposits and melts the sulfur. It can then be pumped out.

Porous, lightweight pumice is mined in great quantities in quarries on the island of Lipari.

corrode in water or acids and can withstand temperatures as high as 1,650° F. It is used as insulation.

Basalt isn't the only volcanic stone we quarry, however. Polished slabs of porphyry are sometimes used as a wall covering or as a surface on stairs and terraces. Tough, impact-resistant diabase or dolerite is used for monuments (sometimes called "black granite") and is also crushed for use on roads or in concrete mixtures. Thin plates of phonolite—from Greek phone (sound) and lithos (stone)—produce a ringing sound when you strike them. The ancient Greeks used phonolite to make xylophones—different sized plates produce different notes when you strike them. Long before humans learned how to make glass, they were using a kind of natural glass, obsidian. Obsidian is a hard, brittle, usually jet-black rock, formed when lava cools very quickly. If you hit a piece of obsidian with another rock, rounded chips break off and leave very sharp edges. Humans were already using obsidian during the Stone Age, more than 50,000 years ago. They formed thin sharp arrow- or spearheads by chipping away the edges of thin pieces of obsidian. Today obsidian is sometimes used in jewelry.

Not all volcanic products are hard. A lot of loose material builds

The quarries at Carrara, Italy have supplied fine white marble for centuries. Many famous sculptors have used it to make statues.

up around the kind of volcanoes that erupt violently. Over time, volcanic ash and lapilli solidify into volcanic tuff. This is a relatively soft kind of rock and is easy to shape using chisels and saws. Tuff is sometimes used in building houses.

Pumice is an especially important volcanic product. It is white-gray in color and very soft—you can scratch it with a fingernail, and it even floats. Like obsidian, pumice is formed from lava. Obsidian solidifies quickly, however, and the gases dissolved in it can't escape. In pumice, on the other hand, the gases are released when the eruption spews the lava high into the air. The released gases expand into bubbles, causing the lava to "foam." As a result, the solidified stone has a sponge-like texture

The "Big Hole" of the Kimberly mine in South Africa. This hole has produced more than 6,000 pounds of diamonds.

People also use it as a polishing or scouring agent. Hand soap containing pumice is used wherever hands get particularly dirty—in auto repair shops, for example.

The largest and purest pumice deposits are found on the island of Lipari in Italy. Mount Pelato erupted there 1,400 years ago and covered about one-fifth of the island with loose materials that eventually formed pumice. Today, this pumice is taken from giant quarries, ground into a coarse powder, and shipped throughout the world.

Obsidian is an extremely hard type of rock. When you break it, the pieces have razor-sharp edges. In the stone age humans made arrowheads and knives from chips of obsidian.

Gemstones only sparkle in the light after they have been cut and polished. Cutting and polishing the tiny facets is delicate work.

with many tiny, hollow cavities. This is why pumice is a popular construction material in some places, since this porous structure makes it good insulating material.

It may surprise you to know that diamonds are also a kind of volcanic stone. Diamond is the hardest mineral there is. Diamonds have a very high refractive power—they reflect a lot of light—and they have high dispersion qualities—they separate white light into the colors of the spectrum. High-grade diamonds— ones that are especially clear—are cut and used in jewelry. In the light they glitter and sparkle in all the

Where do diamonds come from?

colors of the rainbow. The rarest diamonds are completely colorless and show no impurities, even under a magnifying glass. These diamonds are also the most valuable. Red, green, blue, and yellow diamonds are almost as costly, however. Because they are so valuable, gem-quality diamonds are not sold by ounces or grams, but by carats. One carat is a fifth of a gram—200 milligrams or about 7/1000 of an ounce.

Most diamonds, however, are a dirty yellow, brown, gray, green, or black. We use these diamonds for industrial purposes, where their hardness is valued— in drill bits, rock saws, and glasscutters. Crushed diamond is used in industrial abrasives and polishes.

Diamonds are pure carbon— the same element that forms dark-gray graphite and black soot. The carbon atoms in diamonds bond together in a special way that gives them their extraordinary features.

Some especially large and beautiful diamonds even have names—the "Star of Africa," for example, or the "Tiffany" and "Hope" diamonds. The largest diamond ever found was the "Cullinan" diamond. When it was discovered in 1905, it weighed 3,106 carats (621 grams—almost 1.5 pounds!). This is much too large for a piece of jewelry. It was therefore cut into 106 separate pieces.

The most expensive diamond in recent history—per carat—was a stone that weighed only 0.95 carats but was a very rare blood-red color. In 1987 it sold for about one million dollars!

The most famous diamond mines are in South Africa. About 130 years ago workers discovered flawless diamonds in a small hill near the town of Kimberly. They started mining the site for its treasures and over the years carted away the entire hill. Today, in its place, is the largest hole dug by humans: the "Big Hole" of the Kimberly mine. It is 1,300 feet deep and almost 1,500 feet across. At one time, it was the vent of a volcano. The diamonds are actually found in volcanic rock fragments called kimberlite or "blue ground." Miners have taken more than 6,000 pounds of diamonds from the "Big Hole" alone.

Searching for diamonds is difficult work. Workers have to dig through about 22,000 pounds of kimberlite to find one gram of diamonds. Many of the diamonds found aren't pure enough or flawless enough to be cut into gemstones. These are used in industry.

Geologists aren't really sure how diamonds are formed. What they do know, is that it takes place deep in the Earth under extreme temperatures and high pressure. Then volcanic eruptions bring them to the surface. For several decades now, we have also been able to make diamonds artificially—from graphite that is heated to about 5,400° F and exposed to enormous pressure. Only industrial diamonds can be created in this way, however. Precious gemstone-quality diamonds occur only in nature; outside of South Africa they are found in Namibia, Liberia, Angola, Australia, Russia, and South America.

The 530.2-carat "Star of Africa" in the British scepter is the largest cut diamond in the world.

The best known deposits of

How were the Earth's mineral deposits formed?

copper, zinc, cobalt, nickel, gold, silver, tin, uranium, tungsten, lead—and other metals— were created by forces stemming from magma. When colliding tectonic plates or other forces push layers of rock from the surface down into the Earth's mantle, it heats up and becomes magma. The rock from the surface often contains water, and this water heats up and rises toward the surface. As it does so, it dissolves metals and minerals from the magma and hot rocks it flows through. As it moves toward the surface and

The Bolivian city of Potosi and beyond it, Cerro Rico. Its silver mines are now exhausted.

cools, it deposits these elements in fine crevices and fissures—either in pure form or mixed with quartz or calcium. Over time, these became "veins" of ore. As a result, mountain ranges with numerous volcanoes are very rich in ores. A good example of this is found in the Andes. The city of Potosi in the Bolivian Andes was the largest and richest community in all the Americas in the 17th century. The

While exploring the ocean, deep-sea submarines discovered mineral-rich hot springs on the ocean floor.

source of its wealth was the volcanic Cerro Rico ("Rich Mountain"). It is made of volcanic rock in which the cooling mineral solutions have deposited silver, among other things. For centuries the Spanish mined this silver and, once each year, they ship the year's production to Europe in their "Treasure Fleet." The silver deposits there have long since been exhausted.

Even today, volcanically active areas of the ocean floor are producing new mineral deposits. Water seeps through crevices and cracks in the ocean floor and rises up again at undersea springs in volcanic zones. On its route through the Earth's depths, hot rocks heat it up to 660° F. It does not boil, however, since the water pressure at depths of more than 6,000 feet is very high. While this water was under the ocean floor, it also picked up acids from volcanic gases. They increase the water's ability to dissolve and absorb other elements. As it seeps through the basalt rock

MINERAL DEPOSITS can be anywhere from a fraction of an inch to several feet thick and can extend for many miles. Some minerals are found almost everywhere, others— like gold and silver—only in specific areas. When mineral deposits occur on the Earth's

surface, rain eventually washes them into rivers and streams. Where the current is slow, heavier particles settle and form alluvial deposits— good places to pan for gold.

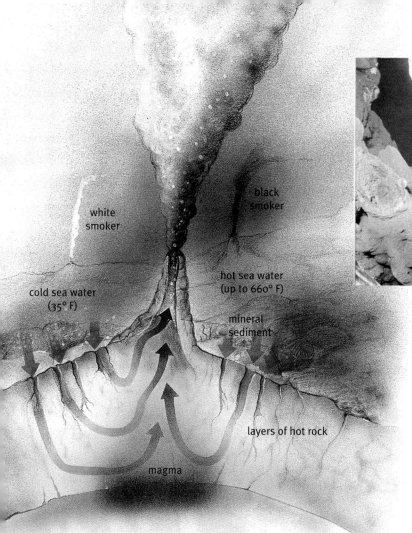

white smoker

black smoker

hot sea water (up to 660° F)

cold sea water (35° F)

mineral sediment

layers of hot rock

magma

When hot water colored by minerals wells up out of undersea springs, we call these springs "smokers."

HOT SPRINGS on the ocean's floor are teeming with life forms. Although the sun's rays never reach them, there are 10-foot-long, bright red pipe worms, white crabs, and shellfish living here. They feed on bacteria, which in turn can live from the sulfur compounds in the water.

of the ocean floor then, this water draws out or "leaches out" mineral elements in the basalt, especially compounds containing manganese, iron, zinc, copper, and cobalt, but also some silver and gold.

If this mineral-rich hot water reaches the ocean floor and comes in contact with the cold ocean water, the metallic compounds are deposited on the ocean floor around the spring as metallic sulfur compounds—usually black in color, but sometimes white, yellow or brown. The water coming from many of these springs is black, like a smoking chimney. This is why they are called "black smokers." Others have a cloudy, milky color and are called "white smokers." These "chimneys" are often many feet high.

Is there a future for geothermal power plants?

There are about 90,000 people living in the capital city of Iceland—Reykjavik—and yet there are hardly any chimneys, even though the city is located north of the Arctic Circle. For centuries the inhabitants of Iceland have heated their homes with hot water and steam from volcanic springs. The steam drives turbines that generate electricity, and the hot water is used to heat homes and greenhouses. Thanks to volcanic heat from the Earth's depths, Icelanders can harvest fresh vegetables and fruit year round—for their own use and for export.

The first geothermal power plant was built in 1904 in Larderello, Italy, south of Florence. It still supplies electricity today. Hot steam is used to generate energy in other countries as well. New Zealand gets about 7 percent of its electricity from geothermal sources. The most efficient geothermal power plant is "The Geysers," located north of San Francisco. More than 300 boreholes

This geothermal power plant is on Iceland. Steam from deep within the Earth supplies electricity and heating.

extending down 1,800 feet supply enough steam to generate 3,000 megawatts of electricity. That is enough for a city of two million inhabitants. Many researchers believe that geothermal energy is a viable substitute for oil and coal. Coal and oil reserves are becoming more and more scarce and won't last forever. The magma in the Earth's depths could supply our energy needs for hundreds of thousands of years.

Extracting geothermal energy is not without problems, however. The steam from the Earth's depths often contains chemicals that corrode or clog pipes. Some of these chemicals are valuable raw materials and the chemical industry can make good use of them. Most of them, however, are poisonous in large quantities. It is very expensive to dispose of them in a way that won't harm the environment.

The biggest problem, however, is that hot steam only rises to the Earth's surface in a few places—where ground water seeps down into layers of hot rock. For years researchers have looked for ways to use the heat from dry hot rock. After all, the energy contained in such rock is about 6,000 times the

energy potential from all known oil reserves. At present, the most promising method is the "hot dry rock" process. Engineers bore two holes into the Earth a certain distance apart and then use blasting to create artificial cracks or connections between the two holes. Then cold water is pumped into one hole. It seeps through the hot rocks into the second borehole and then rises as steam or hot water. This method hasn't been tested enough to show whether it really works or not.

Near Pozzuoli on the Bay of Naples, there

Can volcanologists predict eruptions?

are two big, metal structures in the middle of the white sand at the center of the Solfatara crater. They are radar reflectors. They send data to satellites that are then able to measure the rising and sinking of the ground. Beneath this densely populated strip of land there is a

PREDICTIONS

Volcanologists have achieved a few successes with their monitoring techniques. For example, the number and force of micro-earthquakes increased substantially just before the eruption of Mount St. Helens in 1980. Of course, no one knew that the eruption would be as enormously explosive as it turned out to be.

WARNING SIGNALS are not always reliable, however. In 1984, the port of Rabaul on Papua New Guinea was almost completely evacuated after researchers noted frequent micro-earthquakes and a rise in the Earth of about two feet. Then the forces in the deep suddenly quieted down again without incident.

Protected by a special suit, a volcanologist takes gas and lava samples directly from the vent of a volcano.

giant magma chamber. If pressure in the chamber rises, the ground rises; if it falls, the ground falls.

Geologists take each rise very seriously. If the pressure in the depths increases too much, an eruption might follow. The last time this happened was in 1538, and the eruption created Monte Nuovo—"New Mountain."

For all our technology, however, we are still far from being able to predict eruptions reliably. Scientists

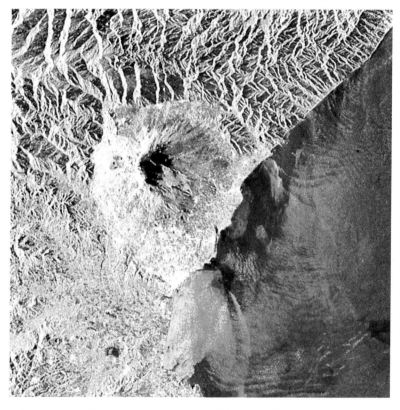

Radar pictures from space—here of Etna—should help volcanologists predict eruptions.

are working on the problem, however, and observatories have been set up on many volcanoes. The first was established in 1811 on Mount Vesuvius. This is where volcanologists work, collecting data about "their" volcano over many years. They note quakes in the ground below, take measurements to catch any rising or falling of the ground, investigate changes in temperature or chemical compositions of gases rising from the vol-

cano, and observe any changes in the crater area or on the volcano's slopes. Many changes they see really can point to an impending eruption. In some cases, seismometers (instruments that measure the intensity of earthquakes) have recorded increased movement in the Earth's depths months before a volcano erupted. We don't feel these micro-earthquakes but the instruments detect them. The number of seismic waves increases from a few per month to a few hundred per day before an eruption. Apparently the pressure of the rising magma opens cracks in the rock. Gas explosions in the molten rock may also play a role.

When magma rises, it lifts the volcano and its surroundings a few inches. For this reason researchers have placed highly sensitive inclinometers (instruments that measure changes in the degree of slope or "inclination") on the slopes of a number of volcanoes.

When magma rises, it also brings heat from within the Earth. The volcano becomes somewhat hotter. We can't feel the slight changes, but satellites with sensitive devices for measuring heat radiation are able to detect even slight rises in temperature.

With modern computers we are now technically capable of monitoring all dangerous volcanoes around the clock—with automatic instruments that transmit data via satellite to central monitoring stations. So far, however, all attempts to establish such a monitoring network have failed because of lack of funds. Thus these mountains remain an ever-present danger for the people who live near them.

Volcanoes around the Globe

EUROPE

Etna (1)

Located on the Italian island of Sicily, Etna is the highest active volcano in Europe with an elevation of 10,902 feet. The earliest eruption for which we have a written record was in 1500 BC, and there have been many minor eruptions since then. The most devastating one was in 1669 and cost 20,000 people their lives. In 1979 an eruption killed 9 people. This hasn't stopped tourists from visiting the site, however.

Beerenberg (2)

The northernmost volcano on Earth is located on the Norwegian island of Jan Mayen, north of Iceland. The 7,470-foot-high volcano has erupted five times since 1633, the last time in 1984.

Hekla (3)

This volcano was known as the "Door to Hell" in the Middle Ages. It has erupted 20 times since 900 AD, each time producing huge lava- and mudflows. Since the area around it is only sparsely populated, there have been few casualties. Hekla has an elevation of 4,890 feet. Its most recent eruption was in 1981.

Laki Fissure (4)

This is a 15-mile-long fissure on Iceland. It holds the record for the amount of lava produced during an eruption—2.8 cubic miles during a powerful explosion in 1783. It filled two valleys and covered almost 200 square miles of land. Nearly all the cattle on the island died, since gases released by the volcano killed the grass in their pastures. 10,000 people died of starvation—about one-fifth of the population.

Teide Peak (5)

This volcano is located on the island of Tenerife. Its Spanish name is Pico de Teide. The mountain is 12,178 feet high and currently dormant. It formed inside the huge caldera of a much older volcano. This dramatic landscape is called "canadas" and is a popular tourist site. A cable car leads to the peak. From here you can see black bands of rugged lava running through the yellow-brown rock of the canadas—evidence of earlier eruptions. There are also traces of volcanic eruptions on the other Canary Islands, particularly Lanzarote and La Palma.

Santorini—also called **Thera** (6)

In 1500 BC a volcano erupted where this Greek island group is now located—north of Crete. The tremendous force caused the ground to cave in and an underwater caldera was formed. The present-day islands

ASIA

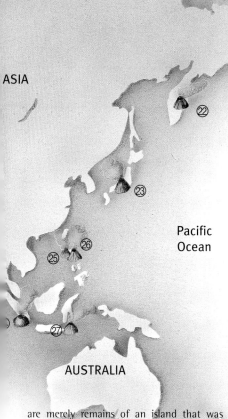

Pacific
Ocean

AUSTRALIA

are merely remains of an island that was once much larger. Ash from the explosion drifted as far as Egypt, and huge waves devastated the surrounding islands (for example, Crete), and the city of Akrotiri on Thera. The volcanic forces are still active today.

Stromboli (7)
This volcano on an island north of Sicily has an elevation of 3,038 feet. Its nickname is "Lighthouse of the Mediterranean," since it has erupted almost continuously for the past 2000 years—nearly every half-hour.

Vesuvius (8)
This volcano—probably the most famous in the world—is located near Naples, Italy. It is 4,198 feet high. Its most devastating eruptions were in 79 AD (12,000 dead) and 1631 (4,000 dead). The eruption in 79 AD destroyed the Roman cities of Pompeii and Herculaneum, among others. The present-day Vesuvius formed in the caldera of a previous volcano (Mons Vesbius). Vesuvius tends to erupt many times in a short period and then lie dormant for centuries. The last eruption was in 1944, and it has been quiet since then. Today, many tourists climb to the edge of its crater.

Vulcano (9)
The volcano that gave its name to fire-spewing mountains in general is located on a small island north of Sicily. The Romans believed this mountain contained the forge of the fire god, Vulcan.

NORTH AND SOUTH AMERICA

Cotopaxi (10)
This 19,347-foot-high mountain in Ecuador last erupted in 1942. It is still very active, however. It has erupted more than 50 times since 1532. Melting ice from its peak occasionally causes mudflows that reach as far as 60 miles away.

El Chichón (11)
This volcano in southern Mexico became famous in 1982 when it erupted violently—the biggest eruption of the 20th century. Prior to this it had been quiet for centuries. When the 7,300-foot-high mountain erupted, it hurled huge amounts of dust and sulfuric acid into the air. 2,500 people died.

Fernandina (12)
The most active volcano on the Galapagos Islands off the Pacific coast of Ecuador is a shield volcano whose peak has collapsed into a caldera. It probably formed over a hot spot.

Kilauea (13)
This secondary crater of Mauna Loa on the main island of Hawaii is almost constantly active. Its current elevation is about 5,000 feet. Since the lava it discharges is freely-flowing alkaline lava, you can approach it and observe its lava flows and lava lakes without danger of violent eruptions.

Mauna Loa (14)
The biggest—though not the highest—active volcano on Earth is located on the main island of Hawaii. It rises 13,678 feet above sea level. Measuring from the ocean floor, this huge shield volcano is almost 30,000 feet high. Since 1832, almost one cubic mile of lava has flowed out of its craters and fissures and yet it has caused little damage.

Mount Pelée (15)
In 1902, this volcano on the Caribbean island of Martinique spewed out an avalanche of searing, poisonous gases and red-hot ash. It raced down the mountain and destroyed the island's capital, St. Pierre. It killed 28,000 people. There have been other explosive eruptions since then, most recently in 1932.

Mount St. Helens (16)
This Pacific Coast volcano in Washington State erupted in a gigantic explosion in 1980, blowing away the northern slope of the mountain and reducing its height by 1,200 feet. Fifty-seven people died, 230 square miles of forest were destroyed, and a 17-mile-long valley was filled with mud. The most recent eruption was in 1986. Today the mountain has an elevation of 8,360 feet.

Nevado del Ruiz (17)
This volcano in Columbia made headlines in 1985 when a tremendous explosion melted much of the ice on the peak of this 17,716-foot-high mountain. The resulting mudflows rushed down the slopes and covered several towns, including the town of Armero. It killed 25,000 people.

Ojos del Salado (18)
The highest active volcano in the world is located on the border between Chile and Argentina and is 22,560 feet high.

Poás (19)
This volcano in Costa Rica has two crater lakes. It has erupted more than 20 times since 1834. An eruption in 1910 shot a fountain of water 2.5 miles into the air.

Popocatépetl (20)

This massive snow-covered volcano towers above the landscape south of Mexico City. It has had several minor eruptions since its last big one in 1720. It erupted again in 1994 and has been continuously active since then.

Villarrica (21)
This volcano in central Chile erupts at irregular intervals. In 1971, 15 people died when melting ice caused mudflows.

ASIA

Bezymianny (22)
This volcano—formed from several peaks—is located on the Russian peninsula of Kamchatka and is part of the "Ring of Fire" that circles the Pacific. In 1956, a mushroom-shaped cloud rose more than 20 miles into the sky, and pieces of rock fell more than 15 miles away. It left behind a caldera 1.3 miles across. Since the area is practically uninhabited, the eruption didn't cause any deaths. The red-hot ash settled in a near-by valley and heated the ground water. Since then volcanologists call it the "Valley of Ten Thousand Smokes of Kamchatka." There is a similar valley near Katmai volcano in Alaska.

Mount Fuji (23)

This sacred mountain of the Japanese is located on the island of Honshu. It is Japan's highest mountain with an elevation of 12,388 feet. Its crater is 500 feet deep and 1,900 feet wide. It last erupted in 1707.

Krakatoa (24)

This volcano in the Sunda Straits between Sumatra and Java became famous through the biggest explosion in historical times. The eruption on August 7, 1883 completely destroyed the island. The explosions could be heard 3,000 miles away. Most of the 36,000 people killed died in the immense tidal waves caused by the explosion. Devastating effects were felt thousands of miles away.

Pinatubo (25)

When this volcano in the Philippines erupted in 1991, the hot ash and mudflows it generated took 750 lives and caused about 700 million dollars in damages. About 1.2 million people had to leave their homes. The cloud of ash, which was 13 miles high, circled the Earth and caused temporary climate changes.

Taal (26)

Taal volcano is located in the Philippines. It now consists of a large lake that fills the 18-mile wide caldera. A newer vent has formed an island in the middle of this lake. It has erupted at least 30 times since 1572, often accompanied by powerful explosions and tidal waves, and has claimed many lives. When water from the lake flows into the vent, it causes tremendous explosions.

Tambora (27)

In 1815, this volcano on the Indonesian island of Sumbawa hurled out about 19.2 cubic miles of volcanic ash. It was the most powerful eruption in history up to that time and caused tidal waves that killed about 10,000 people on the surrounding islands. The cloud of ash darkened the Sun and caused severe crop failure in the Northern hemisphere, resulting in the starvation of another 80,000 people.

AFRICA

Kilimanjaro (28)

This mountain in Tanzania grew out of three volcanoes and has three peaks. The highest is Kibo Peak, which has an elevation of 19,340 feet. This peaceful volcano is the highest mountain in Africa.

Nyiragongo (29)

This layer volcano in the eastern part of Congo has erupted about 15 times since 1884. In 1977, a fissure opened up on its southern slope and discharged a sea of glowing lava. The molten rock flooded large areas at speeds of up to 45 miles per hour. It killed 300 people.

ANTARCTICA

Mount Erebus (30)

Earth's southernmost active volcano is located on Ross Island. Its 12,280-foot peak is covered with eternal snow, but inside it is a sea of hot magma 328 feet across.

Index